BLACKS
AND
JEWS IN
AMERICA

BLACKS AND JEWS IN AMERICA

AN INVITATION TO DIALOGUE

Terrence L. Johnson & **Jacques Berlinerblau**

The publisher is not responsible for third-party websites or their content. URL links were active at time of publication.

Library of Congress Cataloging-in-Publication Data

Names: Johnson, Terrence L., author. | Berlinerblau, Jacques, author.
Title: Blacks and Jews in America : an invitation to dialogue / Terrence L. Johnson and Jacques Berlinerblau.
Description: Washington, DC : Georgetown University Press, 2022 | Includes bibliographical references and index.
Identifiers: LCCN 2021000054 (print) | LCCN 2021000055 (ebook) | ISBN 9781647121402 (hardcover) | ISBN 9781647121419 (ebook)
Subjects: LCSH: African Americans—Relations with Jews. | United States—Race relations.
Classification: LCC E184.36.A34 J64 2022 (print) | LCC E184.36.A34 (ebook) | DDC 305.800973—dc23
LC record available at https://lccn.loc.gov/2021000054
LC ebook record available at https://lccn.loc.gov/2021000055

∞ This paper meets the requirements of ANSI/NISO Z39.48-1992 (Permanence of Paper).

23 22   9 8 7 6 5 4 3 2   First printing

Printed in the United States of America

Cover design by Spencer Fuller, Faceout Studio
Interior design by BookComp, Inc.

CONTENTS

PREFACE

Of all the theoretically infinite possible relations between different ethnic groups in the United States, the question arises as to why so much is written about the encounter between just two of them. The discourse on the interrelationship between African Americans and Jewish Americans is staggeringly immense, spanning most of the twentieth century and heading into the twenty-first century with expansive force. This relationship has been scrutinized in ways that other intergroup encounters (e.g., Mexican Americans and Irish Americans, Chinese Americans and Italian Americans) have never managed to achieve. A question for us consists of understanding why this particular coupling has produced such a massive body of literature, journalism, scholarly analysis, theological speculation, art, cinema, and poetry, as well as conflict and so forth.

The purpose of this book is to introduce the reader to the complex and contested history of Jewish American and African American relations in the United States. Our inquiry begins by exploring the historical roots of each group's discrete experiences in this country. Then we focus on how they have coalesced sometimes in friendship, sometimes in antagonism, during the past century. Some of the questions we seek to explore are: Do similarities exist between Blacks and Jews that account for the gravitational pull they exert upon one another? Are there differences between them that explain the unique texture of their interaction? How are both related to mainstream White Anglo-Saxon culture in the United States? How do issues of gender and sexual orientation refract the nature of their interaction? How have artists sought to depict their encounters? What political projects have led these groups to form common bonds? And what political projects have placed them in opposition? What role does religion and theology play in Black-Jewish relations? How do questions of homelands—Africa and Israel—figure in their relationship with one another? What do we learn about the very nature(s) of Jewish, Black, and even American identity by scrutinizing the Black-Jewish encounter?

In our individual chapters and conversations, we examine some of the most contested issues that have emerged in the scholarly debates on the encounters between Blacks and Jews. We engage a wide range of literature, film, historical archives, philosophical essays, and newspaper editorials to revisit the complex and diverse issues facing the diverse communities of Blacks and Jews. Our goal is to challenge even the most basic assumption regarding the category of Blacks and Jews—one that assumes all Jews are white.

The 2020 victories of Rev. Raphael Warnock and Jon Ossoff in their Georgia Senate races signal another turning point in the Black-Jewish civil rights coalition. Their intentional effort to build upon the historic relationship between the Reverend Dr. Martin Luther King Jr. and Rabbi Abraham Joshua Heschel opens the door to national and international conversation on the continuing work of what was once called the "Grand Alliance" in the mid-1960s. As with Ossoff and Warnock's work, we believe our book is a call to action—not necessarily to reunite the band but to serve as an invitation to a dialogue on the most fundamental issues facing our democracy and our democratic principles.

1

The Afterglow

JB: Terrence, we started writing this book in the middle of a plague, isolated from our students, colleagues, and extended families and from one another. In the midst of it all, the United States imploded because of yet more senseless killings of African Americans. This violence triggered a multiracial group of citizens to take to the streets in some of the largest protests in American history. Just as we finished the first draft of the manuscript for *Blacks and Jews in America*, Jacob Blake was shot and paralyzed by trigger-happy police in Kenosha, Wisconsin, and two days later a seventeen-year-old white supremacist murdered two people who protested the shooting. We didn't know that any of this would transpire when we started writing the book based on the class we teach together, "Blacks and Jews in America," in 2019.

TJ: The 2020 Black Lives Matter (BLM) protests fundamentally altered the direction of our project—and especially for me personally. The worldwide demonstrations against police killings of unarmed Black men and women were astounding. Likewise, the racial and ethnic diversity of folks who joined in solidarity with Black and Brown protestors chanting "Black Lives Matter!" signaled a dramatic turn in the narrative of anti-Blackness. Almost anyone with a pulse could feel George Floyd's pain through his heartbreaking cry for his deceased mother as a police officer pressed his knee into Mr. Floyd's neck for eight minutes and forty-six seconds on May 25, 2020. The cold silence following Breonna Taylor's death in March of that year also vibrated across the nation and world. For the first time in my life, and probably not since the 1960s when the world witnessed police officers routinely beating Black civil rights workers, no one could deny my people's pain and suffering. Momentarily, the world awakened to Black people's humanity—finally!

But as I watched demonstrators turn the nation upside down, while I was confined to my home with a walking boot on my left foot and a bandaged right knee, I grew frustrated trying to determine the source of the resounding outcry. Why now? And for how long? I don't have an answer to these burning questions. Unfortunately, modern history seems to always look upon African Americans with a crooked smile; short-term victories are almost always swallowed by the devil's advocates. Despite my enduring anger, I cling to the faith of unnamed Black women and men who did not lose their humanity in the face of white supremacy. Their faith and how they translated it into meaningful political action sit at the heart of the historical relationship between Blacks and Jews in North America.

Jacques, what's at stake for you?

JB: Insofar as my son was protesting and insofar as I actually had the very odd, postmodern, once-in-a-lifetime parenting experience of seeing him live on CNN looking as if he had been tear-gassed, or stoned (or both?), the protests hit home in all sorts of ways. I have always had a certain pride in this country, maybe unexamined, and I certainly have not publicly professed it in too many places. It's been sort of like, we can course correct, and we are going to get better. "Pessimism of the intellect, optimism of the will!" as Antonio Gramsci (or Benedetto Croce) said.

But those scenes, starting with the murder of George Floyd, proceeding to that bizarre press conference with the county attorney in Minneapolis (Mike Freeman, I think his name was), and followed by the brutalization of protestors and, of course, President Donald Trump's power-prance through Lafayette Square with the Bible as shield—all of that led to a reckoning about what America actually is. When I shared my observations with Black colleagues, many said, as kindly as they could, "You just figured this out now?"

TJ: Jacques, as you may recall, we spoke often during the height of the demonstrations, and I routinely recounted to you the same refrain: White communities were mostly silent in July 2014 when Eric Garner in New York City gasped, "I can't breathe." Then when Sandra Bland simply asked a belligerent white police officer, "Why am I being pulled over?" on July 10, 2015, she was arrested and died mysteriously three days later in jail. Protestors didn't storm the streets en masse to decry Bland's death, unlike what we witnessed after the killings of Floyd and Taylor.

So I repeat: Why now?

JB: I don't have a good answer. Certainly the coronavirus disease (COVID) lockdown was a factor; it made people focus, because so many were sequestered in their homes. But I'm not sure why so many whites suddenly became engaged, even outraged.

What's interesting, Terrence, is how many "Blacks and Jews" issues surfaced while all of these distressing events took place in the summer of 2020. For example, the Jewish mayor of Minneapolis, Jacob Frey, was booed out of an event when he said he couldn't commit to defunding the police.

TJ: There was also Nick Cannon, who experienced backlash in July 2020. When former Public Enemy rapper Professor Griff (Richard Griffin) said on Cannon's radio show that Jews control the media, Cannon agreed and retorted, "We're just speaking facts."

JB: On the brighter side, I think of the ultra-Orthodox Jews in Crown Heights, Brooklyn, who protested on behalf of Black Lives Matter. Given the fraught history of Blacks and Jews in that neighborhood, this was a very promising development.

TJ: We also should note that BLM cofounder Alicia Garza, who is Jewish, played a major role in designing the architecture of today's progressive politics. Likewise, the passing of Congressman John Lewis in July 2020 prompted the national media to reflect on the relationship between Blacks and Jews. Along with his substantial civil

rights platform, Congressman Lewis was remembered for solicit-
ing assistance in 1960 from Jewish students at Vanderbilt University
with the sit-ins of the Student Nonviolent Coordinating Committee
(SNCC) and for cofounding in 1982 the Atlanta Black-Jewish Coalition, which called attention to what some have referred to as the
"Grand Alliance" of Blacks and Jews during the civil rights movement. During the brief news cycle, the national media and Twitter
turned their attention to the historic encounters between Blacks
and (white) Jews: the founding of the National Association for the
Advancement of Colored People (NAACP) and the National Urban
League (NUL), and the work of educator and civil rights leader
Booker T. Washington and Jewish philanthropist Julius Rosenwald.
The men's collaborative effort established more than five thousand
schools for Black children in fifteen states in the South.

JB: As the summer of 2020 progressed, we also learned more about
Senator Kamala Harris, who is married to a Jewish American! Joe
Biden's naming her as his running mate raised the specter of Blacks
and Jews (and Indian Americans) on Observatory Hill, the vice president's residence in Washington, DC.

TJ: While writing this book amid this upheaval and calls for change,
we also had the opportunity to reassess our work. Whenever friends
ask me to describe to them our course, "Blacks and Jews in America," they all raise two similar questions: Why do you teach this
course? And what do you gain from it?

Jacques, I will ask you a similar question: Do you have any personal connections to the subject matter?

JB: I think so. I was conceived in Paris but was born in Maine and
grew up in Brooklyn, New York. My immigrant mother was very
taken by Martin Luther King Jr. (MLK). It's something she was
nondidactic about, so it took me years to piece together how consistently his name came up in our discussions when I was a child.
She'd casually mention him to me here and there. As I recall, her
key themes were (1) African American folks had it rough here, and

(2) they deserved lots of respect for dealing with insane bigotry. Did my mother know Malcolm? No. She probably still doesn't know about Malcolm X. It was all MLK, who I guess was a sensation in the French media. Also, her English was terrible, so the only people she could speak to were Haitians in the neighborhood. They were her portal to America.

Brooklyn is a great Black city. Brooklyn is also a great Jewish city. Blacks and Jews milling about, side by side, seems normal to me. When I started my teaching career in the City University of New York system, I was teaching mostly Black and Jewish students.

Eventually I moved to Washington, DC, and I was like, "Where did all the Blacks and Jews go?" At least the side-by-side aspect, I miss it, and maybe that's why I teach this course. Along the way, I had a jazz apprenticeship, which taught me everything I need to know about the value of work.

What about you, Terrence? Do you have any personal interest in this, or is it more of a pure scholarly pursuit?

TJ: My connection to Blacks and (white) Jews dates back to the Old Testament stories I read and debated in Sunday school in northeastern Indiana. I was told Africans were entangled in the history and bloodlines of David, Abraham, and Solomon. I also knew Jews claimed the same lineage, but that was the extent of my firsthand knowledge of white Jews.

I don't remember attending school with Jewish kids or living near any Jewish families. Everyone in my immediate world was either a German Lutheran or a Black migrant from the South. Growing up in a small, rural city in Indiana, no one in my immediate world—neither family nor community members—talked about Jews directly.

Strangely enough, I recall a renowned columnist of my hometown newspaper, the late Betty Stein, whom I met when I interned at the paper, but no one ever talked about her being Jewish. I came to know her identity by reading her columns.

Years later I discovered that Indiana's oldest synagogue dates back to 1848 and is in my hometown, which is known as the City of Churches.

Then, when I went off to Morehouse College, I was shocked to stumble upon white professors at a place where I assumed everyone would be Black. In time, I would get to know them, and many of them were Jewish.

JB: So it seems you had very little face-to-face, person-to-person contact with Jewish people as a young man.

TJ: It was not until years later, when I joined the faculty at Haverford College, that I could understand my experiences within a broader historical context and critically reflect upon them. The idea that I could grow up without any direct knowledge of the Jewish community, which was interwoven in the lives of many African Americans and my own family as our physicians, grocers, teachers, and neighborhood shop owners, is a travesty. It also symbolizes the invisibility of Jews in seats of power and their deep influence in Black America, a historical reality linked to broader domestic and international concerns.

At Haverford College, I found my passion for this scholarly work in a reading group I directed called something like "Israel, Palestine, and Ethical Deliberations." A white Jewish student from Dayton, Ohio, and a Palestinian student from New York created the syllabus for what would become tough, critical, and honest conversations on how to deal with the mess we've inherited. From that moment on, I wanted to emulate the moral and intellectual courage I witnessed in the reading group. The subject "Blacks and (white) Jews in America" is an extension of the many complicated issues we explored in the Haverford reading group on Israel and Palestine.

JB: Our original plan in writing this book was that it would be a follow-up, in a sense, to the important 1995 conversation between Professor Cornel West and Rabbi Michael Lerner titled *Jews and Blacks: A Dialogue on Race, Religion, and Culture in America.*[1] How do you think we are different from these two important figures?

TJ: Cornel West is a hugely important figure in my own intellectual development. In fact, his scholarship carved out a path in the academy for uncounted numbers of African Americans and members of other racial ethnic groups. I often use his theologically inspired pragmatism as a starting point for framing my scholarly questions. What I construct in conversation with his body of work is far more humanist and African inspired than what is evident in West's imagination. Whereas West employs a prophetic Afro-Christianity to frame his approach to what he calls the "tragic-comic sense of life," I turn to Africanist-inspired traditions of conjuring, hoodoo, and divination to reconstruct and reimagine Black religion's role in politics, behind what W. E. B. Du Bois characterized as "the veil of blackness."

JB: Please tell our readers just a bit about the idea of the "veil of blackness."

TJ: The veil of blackness is a discourse that prevents whites from seeing Blacks and Black bodies as human, normal, and ordinary.
How are you different from Rabbi Lerner?

JB: Well, first, I am not a rabbi. Nor am I really a man of the Left (or the Right). The rabbi could be very righteous—Torah thunder and all that. I cannot lower that boom. I guess the biggest difference is that, as a secular scholar, my mind tends to gravitate to paradox and irony, whereas the good rabbi understandably inclined to social justice, the Torah, and God's love. I'm really uncomfortable analyzing problems in theological terms, and for that reason I have less legitimacy to speak "on behalf of" Judaism. I'm just one Jew—a free-floating Jew.
Rabbi Lerner and Professor West were dialoguing in the mid-1990s. From the Black-Jewish angle, how is that moment different from our very turbulent period in American history?

TJ: West and Lerner faced a different, though arguably similar, set of social circumstances than what confronted us in the spring of 2020. Their conversation framed itself in relation to Minister Louis Farrakhan's resurgence in the 1990s. As African Americans scrambled to recover from nearly a decades-long attack by Reaganomics, a series of Republican cutbacks to education and social services, and a soaring crack cocaine epidemic, Minister Farrakhan surfaced with a ferocious attack on anti-Black racism and American imperialism. His bold, fiery public sermons offset the sting from debates over affirmative action vis-à-vis Jews and the publication of *The Bell Curve* (Richard Herrnstein and Charles Murray). What emboldened the conversation was the Nation of Islam's publication of *The Secret Relationship between Blacks and Jews* (1991), which argued that Jews financially benefited from anti-Blackness, slavery, and Jim Crow segregation.[2] The major Jewish groups indicted the book, identifying antisemitic tropes that they feared would stoke a civil war between Blacks and white Jews.

The moment was ripe for West and Lerner's conversation. They reclaimed a theological trope of redemption to underscore the unique historical engagement between Blacks and white Jews.

We take a different route to achieving a similar goal of cross-cultural dialogue. Instead of turning to theology, we are guided primarily by cultural criticism and critical race theory. By the latter, I mean an interdisciplinary approach to disentangling race and gender from white supremacist ideology.

What difference do you see in Black-Jewish dialogues between 1995 and 2020?

JB: For one, critical race theory and its refusal to overlook white supremacy as a key variable in scholarly analysis has an academic salience in 2020 that it did not in 1995. Like many scholars, I am wrestling with its implications. Too, there's a lot less sentimentality about Blacks and Jews nowadays. Only older African American and Jewish American folks wax nostalgic about the so-called Grand Alliance. At their moment in time, Lerner and West did not have the benefit of the massive corpus of scholarship that you and I can access, one that teaches us how complex this relationship actually is. So in 2020, I sense far more pessimism about the Black-Jewish relationship—that is, what it did and what it can do.

Connected to that pessimism is a feeling among progressive and liberal Jews of total frustration with the direction taken by the state of Israel. A quarter century ago, before the assassination of Israeli prime minister Yitzhak Rabin in November 1995, there was greater optimism about the prospects for peace with Palestinians. Today, on the Jewish side, the Center-Left is concussed and numb. It doesn't mean they've given up; it just means they've had a very rough couple of decades.

As we share this book with our readers, what are your hopes about what we'll be able to do, and what do you think are the limitations and challenges that confront us?

TJ: Black folks have long given up on an alliance with white Jews—at least this seems to be the case in the scholarly writings and essays I utilize in my courses. White Jews are present but invisible within the familiar and social structures of most African Americans. Without any hesitation, the majority of Black students who enroll in our classes do not express any interest in developing an alliance with white Jews. Their experiences are informed by Jewish assimilation into white, middle-class social groups and by Jewish flight from communities of color.

I don't believe the students' disinterest stems from discontent; instead, it symbolizes the shifting interests among today's Black activists. Unencumbered coalition-building has been bracketed. What is framing today's political vision among Black progressives is intersectionality politics, political platforms based on the intersections of race, gender, class, and sexuality. What we see here is a direct challenge to liberalism's emphasis on individual rights and notions of equal opportunity and equal access.

As you well know, white Jews have benefited from liberalism in ways unimaginable to African Americans. Blacks and Jews must confront this tragic history, which I explore in chapter 3, "Liberalism and the Tragic Encounter between Blacks and White Jews," before any coalition or "reunion" can materialize. The strange irony, however, is that if you want to understand America and its so-called liberal promises, you must engage the history of Blacks and Jews in the United States.

JB: So do you think the discussions that we are about to engage in occur in the "afterglow" period of Blacks and Jews dialogue? Do you think we're surveying something that may have ossified a bit? Are we gazing at something fascinating but something preserved in amber?

TJ: Yes, we're experiencing at this historical moment a lingering nightmare from the unrealized aspirations of Blacks and Jews who believed in liberalism's dreams and the promises of capitalism during the civil rights movement: White Jews benefited; Blacks did not. This point will come up throughout our conversations in this book.

As we detangle this moment, I think intersectionality allows us to see more clearly the structural limitations of thinking through anti-Blackness in the white-Black binary. It pushes us to the messy roots of our problem.

JB: As I argue in chapter 2, "Finding Our Affinities: An Overview of 'Blacks and Jews' Dialogue," intersectionality is very hard on Jews; it's not the framework that's likely to generate dialogue. And you're right: African American activists are increasingly working in this framework. Some theorists are going to have to work through the critique of scholars such as Jessica Greenebaum, David Schraub, and Balázs Berkovits on intersectionality and see if it can be deployed in a way that doesn't ring the fight-or-flight bells of Jews.[3] You haven't given up, however, on the value of this relationship for purposes of education. You concur that by looking at the Black-Jewish relationship, any American—even if not Black or not Jewish—can learn something about this country? Is our encounter, therefore, *generalizable*; that is, does it retain insights for *non*-Blacks and *non*-Jews?

TJ: Definitely. Going back to the classic James Baldwin piece "Negroes Are Anti-Semitic because They're Anti-White," we see that the roots of racism and antisemitism can be traced to white Christianity and its intricate role in sustaining the political lifeblood of the nation.

JB: I agree that this messy, tensile, and very complicated relationship between Blacks and Jews is of much broader interest. As you well know, many of our Asian American students tell us how fascinated they are by this class.

> **TJ:** Great point. Look at what impedes almost every other ethnicity or group of color in the United States. Those impediments point back to what Blacks and Jews have struggled with since their encounter in the New World—the denigration of their bodies, the beliefs that dehumanize them, and so on. More specifically, the idea that Blacks and Jews are non-Christian and non-white—and that they bring in rituals of community and tradition that threaten, I think, the liberal model of individualism—is at the heart of the political imagination of this nation.
>
> What are you hoping to achieve and what do you wish to avoid in this book?

JB: Well, I hope to push back a bit on your critique of liberalism. I'm not ready to abandon the liberal project—not unless we identify better alternatives—because conservatism and its fringe-y, populist excrescences are decidedly not attractive alternatives right now! Maybe you'll sell me on some radical possibilities? I'm an open-minded sort. I really want to dialogue with you about critical race theory and intersectionality. These ideas hover above all our conversations, and I find them fascinating, intellectually challenging, and, obviously, subject to criticism.

Too, I want us both to reflect—as we often have in class—on Afro-Jews and their significance for this dialogue. Maybe they can help us escape from the amber? Because I have written so much about secularism and since you are a scholar of religion, also I selfishly want to ask you a few things about the African American Church and this most complicated "ism."

In terms of what I hope to avoid, I hope to avoid thoughtlessness and empty rhetoric. Sometimes when people are doing a Blacks and Jews dialogue in public (as opposed to in writing), it devolves into a sort of public performance. There are a lot of platitudes and a lot of head nods, too much nodding of the head.

TJ: I think we push against those trite narratives of the Grand Alliance between Blacks and Jews by showing how both groups have struggled, at different points, with many of the fundamental values attributed to this country: religion and secularism, faith and reason, gender and race, and liberalism and capitalism—all of which we discuss. What we've framed is a far more nuanced account of the ideas, traditions, and ideologies that emerge from the struggles and anxieties within the relations between Blacks and white Jews.

As for the "nodding of the head," have you experienced this personally?

JB: Yes, and you were there as well! A few years back, you and I were speaking on a panel sponsored by a major Jewish organization, and I had two sudden insights, epiphanies actually. The first was that few people in that audience (mostly white that day) had any interest in anything I was saying. They wanted to hear from you and another African American panelist, a woman. That was cool! I had no problem with that. I, too, was more interested in what you two were saying.

But the second thing I noticed was more vexing to me—and I've seen this in a lot of these performances, no matter who the audience: Platitudes are spouted. People nod their heads. And then they nod their heads some more. And then someone says, "We're all in this together." Or someone mumbles something about education, the internet, and the youth.

That drives me crazy. It's not that I am looking for brawls and scrums; I actually dislike that as well. But there was a shallowness to the dialogue. I wonder if that was because the dialogue is all these two groups presently possess. So it's easy to smile, argue a bit, nod heads; then go home; and never see one another until the next dialogue.

TJ: I remember the conversation well; it was cordial but not remarkable. The usual topics surfaced: civil rights movement, Black Power, Jewish assimilation, and young African American activists. The mostly white audience hailed from major Jewish organizations, the usual suspects for rehearsing past Black and Jewish relationships.

In light of BLM and the aftermath of COVID-19, we can't return to a dead past anymore. The challenges we face demand an invigorated political imagination and a willingness to struggle for humankind and the planet. A dialogue is necessary, but if it's not connected to a shared commitment to an emancipatory politics or political vision, we will remain bitter, divided, and distorted by our middle-class blues.

Notes

1. Lerner and West, *Jews and Blacks: A Dialogue.*
2. Nation of Islam, *Secret Relationship.*
3. Greenebaum, "Placing Jewish Women"; Schraub, "White Jews"; and Berkovits, "Critical Whiteness Studies."

2

Finding Our Affinities in a "Blacks and Jews" Dialogue

Jacques Berlinerblau

> The fact of the matter is that in neither group is there any-
> thing like a consensus on anything, least of all on each other.
> Nevertheless, they both represent groups within which there
> exists a wide variety of opinion on almost everything, includ-
> ing themselves.
> —Harold Cruse, "My Jewish Problem and Theirs"

"Blacks and Jews" is the catchall scholars use to describe the long and complicated historical relationship between two of America's most dynamic minority groups. As far as catchalls go, it leaves much to be desired. For starters, as Yvonne Chireau and Nathaniel Deutsch point out, these identities "are not mutually exclusive."[1] The rapper Drake is Black and Jewish; as is the comedian Tiffany Haddish; as is the cofounder of Black Lives Matter, Alicia Garza; as is the jurist Lani Guinier; as are hundreds of thousands of other people in the United States.[2] Further, the term "Blacks and Jews" obscures a recurring theme, or accusation, that has surfaced over a century of dialogue and research—that is, Jewish Americans are now racially categorized as white and have enjoyed all the benefits of whiteness. And they have indulged its pathologies too.[3]

This brings us to another shortcoming of the phrase "Blacks and Jews": it lacks a verb. It thus fails to properly illuminate what precisely

Blacks and Jews *do* with one another. The question is deceptively difficult to answer. Are Blacks and Jews having a dialogue, an interaction, a
seminar, a dialectic, a competition, an argument, an estrangement, an
annulment? They have done all of those things. And because the communities are diverse and filled with exceedingly opinionated people, all
of those things have often happened simultaneously. One literary theorist coined the neologism "blackjewishrelations," an ironic allusion to
a phrase that "is being asked to do too much work."[4]

Yet whatever it is that Blacks and Jews do with, or to, one another,
one cannot deny the astonishingly *productive* nature of their encounter.
Their interaction has resulted in the creation of a major civil rights
organization in the form of the NAACP and landmark legislation ranging from *Brown v. Board of Education* to the Voting Rights Act of 1965.[5]
It has produced an immense quantity of think pieces, memoirs, and
reflections by non-Jewish Blacks, white Jews, and Black Jews.

Copious scholarship about Blacks and Jews is found in nearly every
discipline of the humanities and social sciences. No one scholar could
master this capacious bibliography. There is so much research on this
subject that there could be a Department of Blacks and Jews Studies at a
university near you, assuming universities near you don't soon become
business and STEM (science, technology, engineering, and mathe-
matics) schools.[6] This research is almost uniformly readable, thoughtful,
and of high quality. Given that maybe 98 percent of the studies about
Blacks and Jews are written *by* Blacks and Jews, it's almost as if an element of communal pride is at play; when speaking to each other, we
don the prose equivalent of our Sabbath finest.

Then there's all that art—everything from Cannonball Adderley's
cover of *Fiddler on the Roof*, to Grace Paley's "Zagrowsky Tells," to jazz
clarinetist Don Byron's loving reanimation of the Mickey Katz song-
book, to Anna Deavere Smith's performance piece *Fires in the Mirror*, to
Bernard Malamud's *The Tenants*, to Paul Beatty's *Tuff*, to Alice Walker's
Meridian, to Spike Lee's *BlacKkKlansman*, to the Safdie brothers' *Uncut
Gems*, and so much more.[7]

If one were to mix and match any two ethnic groups in the country,
be they Korean Americans, Irish Americans, Italian Americans, Mexican Americans, Indian Americans, Chinese Americans, and so on, it

would become evident that no coupling has generated anywhere near the content of the Black-Jewish engagement. It is likely, in fact, that all of the imagined pairings *combined* wouldn't equal what these two minorities have generated on their own.

Nor has any coupling replicated their degree of rancor. One thing that Blacks and Jews do indeed do is argue. They have argued about Israel/Palestine. They have argued over affirmative action. They have argued about why liberalism advanced one group's interests but not those of the other (see my colleague Terrence Johnson's chapter 3). They have argued about who has suffered more at the hands of white Christendom. They have argued about the ways in which they are similar and different.[8] They have argued about who has inflicted greater suffering on the other, be it the physical violence endured by Jews (from the Crown Heights riot of 1991 to the massacre at Freddy's department store in Harlem in 1995) or the pervasive structural violence imposed on Blacks by Jews who occupy positions of power.[9] They have argued about who has benefited most from an alliance that stretches back a century.

The third decade of the twenty-first century provides a grim and sunken vantage point from which to reflect upon all this. This present moment—post–Charlottesville white supremacist rampage, post–Charleston Emanuel African Methodist Episcopal (AME) Church slaughter, post–Pittsburgh Tree of Life Synagogue massacre, post-pandemic, post–January 6 insurrection, post-Trump, and, in light of the continued murder of Black citizens, anything *but* postracial—is as good a time as any to take stock.[10] Remorse licenses us to ask difficult questions, cast doubt on popular narratives, and raise inconvenient facts.

In what follows, I want to introduce readers to the subject of Blacks and Jews. With the benefit of the previously mentioned massive scholarly resources, I want to revisit the most basic questions: When did the relationship of Blacks and Jews begin? Who does and who does not participate in it? What are the enduring themes of this dialogue? Where, and why, has the dialogue broken down? Through all this work, we encounter what I call the "Harold Cruse Principle."[11] As the epigraph for this chapter indicates, we are dealing with complex and diverse communities. It would be wrong to assume unanimity of opinion or action in either community, posing yet another reason to be skeptical of the term "Blacks and Jews."

The "Relationship"

Clayborne Carson Jr., among the most astute observers of Blacks and Jews, once described the two groups as partners in a marriage who "habitually quarrel in public" yet nevertheless "remain in a relationship that survives for reasons that many observers find inexplicable."[12] The metaphor of relationship provides a helpful, but imperfect, way of conceptualizing this encounter. The strengths and weaknesses of this figure of speech come into sharper relief as we try to ascertain when the relationship between these two minority groups began. An inquiry into this question introduces us to a basic principle of Blacks and Jews discourse: For every narrative there is a counter narrative.

In conventional accounts, their relationship is traced to 1909, the year that the National Association for the Advancement of Colored People was founded.[13] Their shared labor and vision in building that storied civil rights organization was the prelude to nearly six decades of intensive cooperation on racial justice issues. It involved major Black organizations (MBOs) such as the NAACP and the National Urban League, and major Jewish organizations (MJOs) such as the American Jewish Committee, the now-defunct American Jewish Congress, and the Anti-Defamation League (ADL), among many others. These institutions formed the backbone of what is known as the Grand Alliance, or the grand coalition, or the civil rights coalition.[14] All of these peaked in a post–World War II "golden age."[15]

Much has been written about why Jewish Americans—ranging initially from the great German banking families to, eventually, those working-class immigrants fleeing Eastern European shtetls—took such an interest in their African American compatriots. Their motivations for doing so have been relentlessly scrutinized, with opinions fanning out across a vast ideological spectrum. Some speak of their altruism and fellow feeling for their African American brothers and sisters.[16] Others, such as Hasia Diner, see Jewish support for Black causes as based on something approximating benign self-interest; by combating racism, Jews could hold antisemitism in check and burnish their credentials as good liberal Americans.[17] Within Black nationalist and separatist circles, a far less generous reading was advanced. Figures such as Malcolm X or Harold Cruse depicted Jews as self-interested, paternalistic, and exploitative.[18]

No matter what the motivation, the dividend of this first collaboration between Blacks and Jews is read in a generally positive way. Sure, they bickered in the back offices of the MJOs and MBOs. Sure, Blacks and Jews wrestled for control between and among themselves for decades.[19] To the world at large, however, the narrative that emerged is that two minorities partnered to greatly expand the civil rights of American citizens. Most in both communities recognize this deliverable as a legitimate accomplishment. If 1909 is where it all began, then the relationship got off to an auspicious start.

Yet throughout the final decades of the twentieth century, a counter narrative suggested a much less cheery first encounter. A few African American activists identified not 1909 but the antebellum period as when and where the relationship commenced. These figures called attention to the role of Jews in the North Atlantic slave trade and as slave owners in the American South.[20] The Nation of Islam's minister Louis Farrakhan furiously leveled the charge, which had a great impact on subsequent Blacks and Jews dialogue. In 1990 Farrakhan told the *Washington Post* that Jews were responsible for "the ships that brought our fathers into slavery."[21] In a 2010 letter to ADL president Abraham Foxman, Farrakhan claimed there is an "undeniable record of Jewish anti-Black behavior, starting with the horror of the trans-Atlantic slave trade." He continued, "Your history with us shows you have been our worst enemy."[22]

The Nation of Islam's indictment is handed down in volume 1 of *The Secret Relationship between Blacks and Jews* (1991). The text advances an argument that soon spread to some quadrants of the Black community and has lodged itself there to this day.[23] While scholars describe *Secret Relationship* as "an incendiary work of pseudo-scholarship" and "a handbook of anti-history," its impact on popular African American thought cannot be gainsaid.[24] Indeed, the Nation of Islam's worldview has pervaded Blacks and Jews dialogue for decades.[25]

Prior to all the ructions generated by Farrakhan, a small body of research—often conducted by Jewish scholars—explored the same issue. After the ructions generated by Farrakhan, even more scholarship was generated in response to the accusations that were grabbing headlines and fracturing already-delicate relations. The findings, both before and after, were consistent and did not generate much controversy among professional historians.

The scholarly consensus all throughout has been that there *were* Jewish financiers of the international traffic in African persons.[26] Their numbers, however, were small. Seymour Drescher remarks, "It is unlikely that more than a fraction of 1 percent of the twelve million enslaved and relayed Africans were purchased or sold by Jewish merchants. . . . At no point along the continuum of the slave trade were Jews numerous enough, rich enough, and powerful enough to affect significantly the structure and flow of the slave trade or to diminish the suffering of its African victims."[27] David Brion Davis speaks of "the marginal place of Jews in the history of the overall system."[28]

As for plantation slavery in the United States, decades of research did not seem to generate much dissensus either. All seemed to concur that Jewish slave owners did exist, yet their numbers were not considerable in the South and were minuscule compared to the overall population of Jews in the United States.[29] Jason Silverman estimates that five thousand Jews owned slaves out of a general population of 400,000 slave owners, making Jews 1.25 percent of all those who engaged in this practice.[30]

Yet the numbers do not tell the whole story. The story is that in their passion for the South and the so-called peculiar institution, Southern Jews as a whole were fairly indistinguishable from their white gentile co-Southerners. Silverman writes that in a hostile environment Jews "could not, or would not, ever become a vocal critic of the institution."[31] "Southern Jews," comments Robert Rosen, "accepted regional customs and institutions, and most significantly, its greatest pathology, slavery."[32] Not surprising, there were no Jewish abolitionists in the South.[33] Scholar after scholar has noted that Southern Jews were avid supporters of the Confederacy, accepting of the peculiar institution, and disinclined to dissent in public. As Bertram Korn famously observed, Blacks were an "escape-valve" for Southern Jews; hatred was

directed to the former, while the latter became "white" by never challenging, and even abetting, that hatred.[34]

The data, as it emerges, is most surprising not to Blacks but to
white Jews. In fact, it would be difficult to describe the perplexity that
afflicts liberal American Jews—or upward of 75 percent of American
Jews—when reading these accounts. Brows furrowed, we ask of our
aforetime Southern coreligionists, Did the hyperconvoluted Judah
Benjamin really serve as the secretary of state of the Confederacy?[35]
Did one Solomon Cohen actually declare that slavery was "the only
human institution that could elevate the Negro from barbarism and
develop the small amount of intellect with which he is endowed?"[36]
Did pro-Confederate agitator Eugenia Levy Phillips so enrage a Union
general in 1862 (by loudly mocking from her New Orleans balcony the
funeral procession of a Union lieutenant) that he had her banished to
an island in the Gulf of Mexico?[37]

In truth, the number of Jews in the entire country opposed to slavery in the antebellum period was likely far larger than the ones alluded
to here and ranged from members of eighteenth-century manumission societies to nineteenth-century abolitionists such as Rabbi David
Einhorn.[38] But still, the very existence of pro-slavery, pro-Confederate
Jews—no matter how small their relative numbers—creates a massive
cognitive disconnect for most contemporary Jewish Americans. This
disconnect exists for a variety of reasons, foremost among them being
that Jews are rarely taught about this chapter in their history. On the
contrary, Jews have been taught to trace a direct, rainbow-colored line
from the foundation of the NAACP in 1909 to those images of Rabbi
Abraham Joshua Heschel marching arm in arm with Dr. King in Selma,
Alabama, in 1965.

The disconnect also exists because the antebellum Southern Jews we
discussed are not the ancestors of most American Jews today. The latter's forefathers and foremothers arrived from eastern Europe between
1881 and 1921 (in fact, even today's southern Jews mostly migrated from
the northern United States).[39] The overwhelming majority of that community grew to embrace positions that ranged from Franklin Delano
Roosevelt's New Deal liberalism, to trade unionism, to socialism, to

outright communism. These vast liberal and left tranches of American Judaism had little fondness for the politics of the Confederacy, white supremacy, the Republican Party, or racist southern Democrats (i.e., Dixiecrats). Most had very little contact with the South (unless one considers Miami the South).

In light of all this, it is hard to answer the following question: Did the relationship between Blacks and Jews start with the founding of the NAACP in the twentieth century or with the Jews who were involved with slavery (or opposed to it) in the antebellum period? But for the sake of fairness and to expose some of the flaws of conceptualizing Blacks and Jews as having a relationship, a different question needs to be asked: Who was the first African American to voice an opinion on Jewish Americans (as opposed to biblical Israelites, Hebrews, etc.)? Not being a scholar of African American history, the best I can come up with is a haphazard response.[40] In 1884 Frederick Douglass remarked, "The Jew was once despised and hated in Europe, and is so still in some parts of that continent; but he has risen, and is rising to higher consideration, and no man is now degraded by association with him anywhere. In like manner the Negro will rise in the social scale."[41] That so little is known about what Blacks thought of Jews illustrates a discursive asymmetry between the two groups that mirrors their discrepant standing in American society.[42]

This reminds us that a fundamental component of the relationship between Blacks and Jews—between Blacks and all groups—in the United States has been the lack of social and economic equality. Even if we date their relationship to the first decades of the twentieth century, we must recognize that this state of inequality thoroughly tinctures their engagement with one another. David Levering Lewis referred to the NAACP in its early years as having "something of the aspect of an adjunct of the B'Nai B'rith and the American Jewish Committee."[43] Adolph Reed Jr. noted that this inequality between the MJOs and MBOs extended forward in time and lamented that "Jewish and Black leadership is acted out on a terrain defined by the former."[44] This inequality certainly strained their first large-scale encounter with one another in the cities of the North.

On the Ground: The Urban Encounter

As the previous section indicates, the overwhelming majority of Blacks and Jews in America had no interaction whatsoever until the twentieth century. It was then that members of both communities collaborated on various civil rights projects. What must be noted is that those people having this vital relationship were elites either by virtue of education, birth, talent, wealth, or some combination thereof.[45] In the words of David Levering Lewis, they were "assimilationist Jews and integrationist Afro-Americans."[46] Lewis suggested that "the Talented Tenth and Negrotarian Jews" both had somewhat complex, even antagonistic relationships with their own poor and working classes.

As for the poor and working classes, their encounters took place in the northern United States in the first decades of the twentieth century. Blacks arrived via continuous waves of settlement known as the Great Migration, which coincided with the previously mentioned surge of Jewish immigration from eastern Europe. Their points of contact were neighborhoods in Boston; New York; Philadelphia; Baltimore; Chicago; Detroit; Washington, DC; and elsewhere.[47]

That these two groups interacted "on the ground" in these commercial and residential spaces is significant. White ethnics inclined to use every means necessary, including violence, to prevent migrating Blacks from coming into proximity with them. Jews were a conspicuous exception to this rule. They almost never devolved into "egg-and-stone-throwing mobs" when Blacks wished to settle in their neighborhoods.[48] In an underappreciated study, B. Z. Sobel and May Sobel broke down the "classic pattern" thusly: "Negroes moved into the areas being vacated by Jews, whose flight then increased (becoming a virtual exodus), leaving behind them primarily the older segments of the population and, very importantly, the small businessmen and landlords, with whom the Negro community had perforce to deal."[49]

That Jews were nonviolent and nonterritorial does not absolve them from the charge of being racist. Many Jews were racist, as evidenced by those who abandoned their neighborhoods when Blacks appeared. Other Jews who lived and worked in close proximity to Blacks were likely racist as well, though their engaging in commerce with Blacks made them unusual when compared with white Anglo-Saxon Protestants and other white ethnics who wouldn't even extend that courtesy.[50] Studies of Jewish merchants in the South in the early twentieth century, be they "'rolling store' men" or small shop owners, consistently show that that they catered to a Black clientele in ways that made them anomalous throughout the region.[51]

Last, there were working and middle-class Jews who shared the commitments of their elite coreligionists in the MJOs and made common cause with African Americans. The proportion of this latter group among American Jews varies according to decade, though my hunch is that one would see spikes in the 1930s and 1940s among Jewish socialists and communists—an encounter that created its own operatic subchapter in the Blacks and Jews dialogue.[52] Further, in the 1950s and 1960s, an immense cohort of Liberal Jews embraced civil rights causes. Alongside them were younger, secular radicals. Reflecting on the tumult of the 1960s, Carson has called attention to a "shared Afro-American-Jewish radical culture" whose roots extended back decades and that was completely "alienated from prevailing white cultural values."[53]

So the point is not to say that Jews were free of racist thoughts and actions—a narrative that many who speak nostalgically about the Grand Alliance tend to promote. In a nation so pervaded by white supremacist worldviews, how could Jews magically evade sharing that prejudice? Rather, the sociologically intriguing fact is their *diversity* of postures toward Blacks. Among those postures was an openness to interaction, and even cooperation, that was exceptional by the contemporary racist standards that prevailed. That cohort, small among Jews but incredibly persistent and durable across time and space, is what made and makes Jews unusual.[54]

Various factors might explain why a significant subset of Jews displayed this more open posture. Like the Blacks they met in the cities, these Jews "in the streets" were themselves traumatized newcomers and, given their ancestors' travails in the Old Country, harbored deep suspicions of coercive state power. These experiences certainly instilled in some Jews a sense of what it felt like to be a powerless "other" (as the Yiddish press's breathless and outraged coverage of lynchings in the South indicates).[55] Factor in that they brought with them a wide range of post-Marxist ideologies, and one can see what made them different from other Euro-ethnics whom Blacks encountered.

Yet we cannot escape the fact of inequality. The relationship of the Jewish American to the African American was one of grocer to customer, teacher to student, welfare worker to client, pawnshop owner to musician, landlord to tenant. These glaring asymmetries on the level of daily encounters tended to create enmity between the rank and file.[56] This inequality extended to the realm of women's interactions as well.

Gender

"When relations between 'blacks and Jews' are talked about," wrote bell hooks in 1992, "what is really evoked is the relation between black men and white Jewish men."[57] The dialogue, hooks continued, "has mainly been an exchange between male thinkers."[58]

In the thirty years since hooks made her observation, there has been a slow, steady increase in the presence of women's voices in Blacks and Jews dialogue and scholarship. Still, the consequences of nearly a century of male-dominated discourse are quite apparent. For example, we do not possess a single comprehensive study that looks at the history of Blacks and Jews uniquely through the optic of gender. By contrast, we have three monograph-length studies of Blacks and Jews in literature.[59]

In any case, the presence of more women's participation has had two noticeable effects. The first has been greater attention to the role of women in this encounter.[60] Earlier we looked at how Blacks and Jews engaged in that acronym galaxy of major MJOs and MBOs. Those organizations have always been of interest to scholars, likely because they leave behind detailed archives and appear in news sources that historians can access. Precisely as bell hooks stipulated, men dominated those interactions. The respective scholarship is also about mostly one gender.

Cheryl Greenberg's extensive research on the MBOs and MJOs, however, points us in the direction of women's organizations, such as the National Council of Jewish Women, the National Association of Colored Women, the National Council of Negro Women, or the Women's Division of the American Jewish Congress.[61] On the more local level, Debra

Schultz in *Going South: Jewish Women in the Civil Rights Movement* studied fifteen Jewish women, mostly northern, who worked with SNCC
in the turbulent 1960s.[62] They stayed right until the purges of whites
from SNCC membership in December 1966 (and were heartbroken by
their dismissal).[63] The stories of these very courageous women are compelling, especially as one realizes the distance these radical individuals
stood from the ever-cautious, centrist MJOs.

Inequality, as we have seen, is a recurring feature of Black-Jewish
encounters, and the domain of gender is no exception. One example is
the treatment of Black domestic workers by Jewish women in the so-
called slave markets. In the 1930s and 1940s MJOs often found themselves fielding complaints from MBOs about Jewish housewives who
hired Black domestic workers at exploitative wages and subjected them
to abusive treatment.[64] In 1935 Ella Baker and Marvel Cooke went
undercover on 167th Street and Jerome Avenue in the Bronx and concluded that "the 'mart' is but a miniature mirror of our economic
battlefront."[65]

The second difference one notices when women conduct Black
and Jewish dialogues concerns tone. Letty Pogrebin complains of the
"power-posturing" of Black and Jewish men who seemed incapable
of "talking personally, exposing their vulnerabilities, and making real
human connections."[66] The author reflects on how she changed her
opinions in a forum "devoted to female-style communication, down-
and-dirty mutual self-disclosure and emotional honesty."[67] In another
piece, Pogrebin charts the rise and fall of her Black and Jewish women's
dialogue group, offering honest reflections on its failures.[68] Interestingly, very few of the issues broached by Pogrebin's group are different
from those we see in male-dominated dialogue (one exception being
Black women's frustration at the high number of white Jewish women
who date and marry African American men).[69]

In an important piece, Barbara Smith engages "the complicated
connections and disconnections between Black and Jewish women."[70]
One of the pleasures of reading this article is her self-critical and self-
reflexive style of reasoning. Smith is acutely aware of how fraught
Black-Jewish dialogues are. She starts by noting, "I am anti-Semitic."[71]
Little in her piece indicates that she is. But her hyperawareness of

where the sensitivities lie for both communities embodies what often distinguishes women's dialogue.

Self-critical and self-reflexive are not the descriptors one might use when looking at parallel dialogues between men. One thinks of Nat Hentoff's all-male volume of 1969 titled *Black Anti-Semitism and Jewish Racism*.[72] Most of the contributors' pieces read as if the men had just returned from some epic Black-Jewish street brawl and wished to share their side of the story.[73] Such was the mood in 1969, after the Six-Day War, the controversies set off by SNCC's anti-Zionist rhetoric, and the Ocean Hill–Brownsville teachers' strike in Brooklyn.[74] Nearly every piece snarls. Almost none of the contributors exhibit the best discursive practices that Smith, Pogrebin, and hooks suggested decades later.

Then again, we ought not essentialize women's discursive abilities. In the long history of Blacks and Jews dialogue, women have engaged in the same dustups and often about the same topics, such as the state of Israel, the Zionist movement, and the question of Palestinian rights. We'll return to this issue, but for now let us register that these tensions surfaced around the first Women's March, which took place on January 21, 2017, and attracted between three million to five million participants in the United States alone.[75] It is considered "likely the largest single-day mass demonstration in recorded U.S. history" and was initially feted as a victory of intersectional activism.[76]

Yet in the immediate aftermath of the event, a familiar script played out. One of the original organizers of the conference, a Jewish American woman named Vanessa Wruble, left the group and cited a pervasive antisemitic atmosphere among its leadership.[77] A witness to the proceedings claims that Tamika Mallory, the event organizer, commented to Wruble: "Your people hold all the wealth."[78] It was also alleged that two of the organizers told Wruble something to the effect that "Jews needed to confront their own role in racism."[79] Much of what transpired between Wruble and Mallory is unclear and disputed, though there were hurt feelings all around.[80]

The whole episode then demonstrated an iron rule of Blacks and Jews controversies: There must be Minister Louis Farrakhan. Mallory, it turned out, was a fan of the controversial Nation of Islam leader and referred to him on Instagram as "the GOAT" (greatest of all time).[81]

And with that, the relationship and the dialogue went right back to all the usual recriminations.[82]

Race: Jewish Whiteness

For nearly the entire breadth of Blacks and Jews dialogue, two themes have recurred with astonishing frequency. The first is that Blacks are antisemitic.[83] The second is that Jews are racist. Perched between these recriminational pillars, like a pale keystone, is a third charge: Jews are white. These claims are triangulated in the most well-known text in the Blacks and Jews canon—James Baldwin's 1967 essay, "Negroes are Anti-Semitic because They're Anti-White."[84] There, the famed author describes Harlem in the 1930s and 1940s as a place of exploitative Jewish landlords, grocers, butchers, pawnbrokers, teachers, welfare workers, and so forth. "The Jew is a white man," Baldwin intoned.[85] "The most ironical thing about Negro anti-Semitism," he continued, "is that the Negro is really condemning the Jew for having become an American white man—for having become, in effect, a Christian."[86]

For all of the dash, forward-hurtling momentum, and certitude of Baldwin's prose, his argument, perhaps intentionally, tends to cast doubts upon itself. Baldwin makes it very clear that he (and other African Americans?) knows full well that Jews are *Jews*, a people with their own tragic history in the iron furnace of white Christendom. He concedes that in the United States, Jews are merely bit players in Black oppression, just "doing their [i.e., the Christians'] dirty work."[87] The implication, however, is that Baldwin (and other African Americans?) overlooks these distinctions because Jews have become, apparently through volition, white. In so doing, they are as racist as all other people of that hue.[88] But if that is so, then why does Baldwin speak of "Negro anti-Semitism"?[89] If Jews are white, why don't Blacks simply hate them *as whites*?[90]

I raise this ambiguity in Baldwin's essay to call attention to the ambiguities that abound on the subject of Jewish whiteness in Blacks and Jews dialogue. Put simply, we—and by "we," I mean Jews, Blacks, scholars, activists, journalists, clergy, laypeople, and so on—are all over the map when it comes to addressing the whiteness of Jews. Not all Blacks agree that Jews are white, not all Jews agree that Jews are white, not all gentile whites agree that Jews are white, and not all scholars agree as to when Jews "became" white. And the incontrovertible fact is not all Jews are white!

To work our way through each of these categories of confusion would be beyond the scope of this chapter. Suffice it to say that the racial assignment of Ashkenazi Jews in the United States has always been in flux. Eric L. Goldstein in *The Price of Whiteness: Jews, Race, and Identity* points out that "Jews defied easy placement into the categories of black and white."[91] His research demonstrates that Jewish Americans have been variously racially configured as Asiatic, or Hebrew, or Semitic, or Caucasian, or White, or something else. Sometimes Jews embraced these identities. Sometimes they contested them furiously.[92] Sometimes different Jews took different positions on these issues at the same time. Cheryl Greenberg has wondered aloud whether "in some inchoate and generally unexamined way, most American Jews have understood themselves as a separate race . . . without being a separate color."[93]

Karen Brodkin sees Jews and other "Euromales" as having become white after World War II.[94] The transition was stimulated by the GI Bill and other government programs (whose largesse was not extended to Blacks) that opened doors for Jewish advancement. Brodkin's study, however, does not factor in southern Jews, and this problematizes her hypothesis. As we have seen, they were *already* granted white status in the antebellum period. But in the twentieth century, when southern Jews espoused communism or supported desegregation, their status as white was reconsidered by groups such as the Ku Klux Klan.[95] The "whiteness" of Jews fluxes across time and space. Jews have become and unbecome white. And become white again.

Even among gentile Blacks who are disappointed in Jews becoming white, one notices a hesitancy to construe them as being fully white. We saw James Baldwin hedging as to what Jews actually were. Harold Cruse, in an account of his own "Jewish Problem," concedes that Jews are a "variant" of white.[96] One survey found that Blacks in the South saw Jews as a "third race."[97] Barbara Smith approvingly invokes the poet Cherríe Moraga, who speaks of Jews as "a colored kind of white people."[98] Yet in the same essay, Smith mentions her frustrations "when white Jewish women of European origin claim Third World identity by saying they are not white but Jewish, refusing to acknowledge that being visibly white in a racist society has concrete benefits and social-political repercussions."[99]

Smith's remark encapsulates a long-running impasse in Blacks and Jews dialogue. Many Jewish Americans will acknowledge that they "pass" as white. They will concede that they are the beneficiaries of white privilege as well. Yet they are left uneasy by a dialogue that starts from those points and never looks back. Intellectuals such as Baldwin and Smith angle the discussion so that it *begins* with the incontrovertible premise that Jews are white. The next step, then, is for Jews is to reflect on how injurious their embrace of that identity has been to Blacks.

Many Jews are willing to do that, but they feel that those fundamental premises need to be qualified as well. They wish to communicate that in being perceived as white, they feel shunted, rather aggressively, into a category they never wanted to inhabit in the first place—a category whose politics and grievances they steadfastly reject with their votes. These Jews also feel far less than safe in their "whiteness" than some critics contend. The historical record of antisemitism teaches us that the standing of Jews within a society is always unstable and vulnerable to rapid decline, scapegoating, and backlash.[100] To understand the Jewish mindset, argues Ellen Willis, one must grasp that they are "permanently insecure."[101] As Saul Bellow intoned of his protagonist, a Holocaust survivor named Arthur Sammler: "Like many people who had seen the world collapse once, Mr. Sammler entertained the possibility it might collapse twice."[102]

A dialogue about Jewish whiteness is absolutely necessary because Jews *have* been able to pass for white and *have* benefited from it at the expense of Blacks.[103] By the same token, white Jewish ambivalence about this status, and the awareness that this status could be suddenly revoked, makes many Jews uneasy about Baldwin's equation. This is where the conversation stalls.

Afro-Jews / Jews of Color

A few decades back, bell hooks remarked that we lack "a complex language to talk about white Jewish identity in the United States and its relationship to blackness and black identity."[104] Just a few years prior, law professor Kimberlé Crenshaw had started developing the concept of "intersectionality."[105] The theory, which soon became immensely popular, focused on the interplay between racism and sexism.[106] Crenshaw averred that "the intersectional experience is greater than the sum of racism and sexism"; therefore, nonintersectional inquiries fail to capture "the particular manner in which Black women are subordinated."[107]

Were we to apply Crenshaw's hypothesis to Blacks and Jews dialogue, we could ask how whiteness and Jewishness intersect. We could ask how those two separate identities synthesize to become something greater than their component parts. We could ask how that new hybrid "white Jewish" identity engages with, and potentially subordinates, Blackness and Black identity. Might this theory provide the "complex language" sought by bell hooks?

I think the answer is no, if only because intersectional theory has peculiar consequences when applied to Jews. Early critics felt it concentrated too narrowly on race, class, and gender. That tight focus diminished two crucial variables for making sense of white Jewish American identity: ethnicity and religion.[108] Intersectionality thus strained antisemitism *out* of the equation, as it did the experience of being non-Christian in a majority-Christian country—variables that Jews do not think are irrelevant. More recent commentators contend that intersectional theory can inadvertently foment antisemitism. As David Schraub notes, "When Jewishness . . . is understood primarily as a subspecies of Whiteness, it obscures important features of Jewish experience for White and non-White Jews alike, while often accentuating or accelerating antisemitic tropes."[109]

Given these concerns about intersectionality, I recommend that a better language, or approach, for a Blacks and Jews discourse is Jewish *diversity*. How do we begin a dialogue on Jewish whiteness? By getting all parties involved to recognize that not all Jews are white. Now is the perfect time to have that conversation.

In recent years, "individuals who self-identified as both black and Jewish have begun gaining national attention and a legitimacy long denied them."[110] In their wake, there has been a proliferation of academic studies about Jews of color in general and Afro-Jews in particular.[111] The latter body of research has introduced us to a vast array of Jews of African ancestry, both nationally and globally. That an Afro-Jewish identity doesn't quite "fit" within standard Blacks and Jews dialogue is increasingly noted. Lewis R. Gordon writes, "I . . . am an Afro-Jew, which places me in a strange nowhere location in the logic of discursive formulations of 'blacks and Jews.'"[112] The recognition of Afro-Judaisms, I believe, is indispensable to the next stage of Black-Jewish dialogue.

For now, let's acquaint ourselves with a few forms of Afro-Judaism. Each has its own complex relation to the white Jewish world. I find it useful to toggle between three distinct vantage points when thinking about this issue. First and foremost, how do these various Afro-Jewish groups relate—or not relate—to white Jews in the United States? Second, how do the overwhelmingly white Jewish American denominations (i.e., secular-humanistic Judaism, Reconstruction, Reform, Conservative, modern Orthodox, and ultra-Orthodox) affirm or deny different types of Afro-Jewish people? Third, if Israeli citizenship is guaranteed to all Jews as defined by the Jewish state and its chief rabbinate, then which types of Afro-Jewish persons are eligible for absorption and patriation via the Law of Return?

Keeping those queries in mind, we briefly survey some major categories of Afro-Jewish identity.[113] To begin, there are the African American *converts* to the previously mentioned Jewish denominations (given the power of the Orthodox rabbinate in Israel, these converts would likely need to be converted in select Orthodox traditions if they wish to obtain Israeli citizenship). A subset would be the children of African ancestry who are adopted by (white) Jewish parents and converted. Then there are the so-called civil rights babies, or children of white Jewish and non-Jewish African American parents.[114] Such "mixed race" individuals are eligible for Israeli citizenship by virtue of having one biological Jewish parent.

Next, we come to groups that, following James Landing, we place under the category of "Black Judaism" (as opposed to "black Judaism"). As Landing defines them, they comprise "black persons [who] identify themselves as Jews, Israelites, or Hebrews (sometimes as Hebrew-Israelites)."[115] Janice Fernheimer points out that the capital *B* implies that these groups are "not necessarily accepted by the recognized Jewish community."[116] These communities arose, and mostly continue to develop, separately from the mainstream Jewish denominations.[117]

Emerging in the Northeast in the period after Reconstruction, Black Jewish groups retained a sizable number of members with roots in the Caribbean.[118] The congregations maintained tensile and complex relations with white American Jews and their institutional bodies.[119] More often than not, they viewed white Jews as impostors who bore no direct relation to the Israelites or Hebrews mentioned in the Bible.[120] White Jews, for their part, exhibited a great degree of curiosity in and fascination for Afro-Jews; however, most did not view them as Jewish according to Halacha, or normative Jewish law.

Many of these Black Jewish communities are "Judaizing," meaning that they originated from Black Protestant communities whose emphasis on the Old Testament ignited their interest in Judaism. They sought, according to Fernheimer, to "be like" Jews but not to become Jews (as represented by white Jews).[121] She uses the phrase "Black Judaizm" to refer to groups that never needed, or wanted, to be recognized by mainstream Judaism.[122]

For complex reasons, sometimes involving living in proximity to white Jews, various Black Protestants at the turn of the nineteenth century gravitated toward Judaism. They often formed their own seminaries and developed their own interpretive traditions, rituals, holidays, and so forth. One thinks, for example, of the Commandment Keepers Ethiopian Hebrew Synagogue in Harlem. The congregation led by Rabbi Wentworth Arthur Matthew emerged in the 1920s. Jacob Dorman speaks of the group's bricolage of elements from "Pentecostal churches and . . . Freemasonry, Jewish Kabbalah, and African American conjuring."[123]

In the 1960s, African Hebrew Israelites emigrated to Dimona, Israel. After a difficult and controversial absorption process, the group has developed thriving communities both there and in the United States.[124] On the extreme fringes are the Black Hebrew Israelites whose members engaged in acts of violence toward Orthodox Jews in 2019.[125]

A different category consists of persons born on the African continent who identify as Jewish. Descendants of Sephardic Jews from the countries of Egypt, Morocco, Algeria, Tunisia, and Libya now live overwhelmingly in Israel. The story of Ethiopian Jews (Beta Israel) and their airlifts to Israel, encounters with racism, and turbulent assimilation is well known.[126] Researchers such as Tudor Parfitt and Edith Bruder have studied African Jewish communities in Ghana, Zimbabwe, Madagascar, Nigeria, and South Africa, among other countries.[127]

Debates about "who is a Jew" make it tricky to quantify the Afro-Jewish population in the United States. Jewish organizations put the figure at a few hundred thousand, though they are likely often looking at a slightly broader "Jews of color" category within the major denominations (which may include, for example, Latinx Jews).[128] A recent study estimated that 12–15 percent of the American Jewish population could be characterized as Jews of color.[129] If we add to that number those groups that self-recognize as Jewish (but are not deemed *Halachically* Jewish), such as the previously noted Black Judaizms, I would estimate that in the United States more than half a million people of African ancestry consider themselves Jews.

Only one blanket statement can be made about all American Afro-Jews: Nearly all report a sense of frustration and disappointment with their white coreligionists. Lewis Gordon notes that many white Jews reflexively—and wrongly—assume that all Afro-Jews were once Christians; thus, the white Jews discount their Judaism.[130] In her memoir, *Black, White, and Jewish: Autobiography of a Shifting Self,* Rebecca Walker recalls "a WASP [white Anglo-Saxon Protestant]-looking Jewish student" who asked her, "Are you really black and Jewish? . . . How can that be possible?"[131] It is rare to read about Afro-Jews who don't share these types of experiences vis-à-vis white Jews.[132] "We've been hurting so long," sighed Rabbi Eliezer Brooks.[133]

The pervasiveness of these charges recommends some serious soul-searching and introspection by white Jews. Interestingly, white Jewish Americans have always looked toward *Christian* African America, be it the churches or the MBOs, as the key partner in Blacks and Jews conversation and action. But why not also maintain a dialogue with as many of the Afro-Jewish communities surveyed earlier as possible? In fits and starts, such dialogues have taken place. Fernheimer has chronicled the pioneering work of Hatzaad Harishon, a group that worked from 1964 to 1972 to bring together Black Jews and mainstream white Jewish communities.[134]

What I am envisioning, though, is a national Jewish conversation about this matter, with all of the resources that such an undertaking requires. Jewish institutions in the United States are renowned for their organizational acumen and their ability to mobilize toward lofty objectives (see the effort to save Soviet Jewry in the 1970s and 1980s or the campaigns on behalf of Darfur in the 2000s). If, in the aftermath of the protests over the murder of George Floyd, we are viewing racism as a national pandemic, then Judaism should as well. A sustained dialogue with different types of Afro-Jews—even those who engage in their own delegitimization of white Jews—would remind white Jews of many things. Namely, it would endow them with a greater sensitivity to the injustices that confront people of color in this country.

If such a sustained, broad dialogue could occur—and it's a big "if"— then possibilities would open up for Blacks and Jews dialogue. Rabbi Capers Funnye, a cousin of Michelle Obama's, has volunteered again and again to perform the function of a bridge in this historic partnership. "Black Jews," suggests the rabbi, "offer a dynamic opportunity to link these communities."[135] Rabbi Funnye is right. A three-way conversation between a gentile Black person, a white Jew, and an Afro-Jew is likely to be very different than one without the latter's presence. As we have seen, non-Jewish Blacks have increasingly concluded that Jews are white. Engaging with persons of African-Jewish ancestry would remind them that more than half of the world's Jewry is not white. Hopefully, it also would remind white Jews in the United States of the same.

Israel/Palestine

I have pointed to accusations of Jewish racism and Black antisemitism as one conversational through line in Blacks and Jews dialogue. Telling white Jews that they are embracing whiteness and thus bolstering white supremacy is not an easy conversational topic for America's Jewish mainstream. Then again, most in this overwhelmingly liberal community understand the value of self-criticism and self-correction. While the subject may discomfort them, it doesn't necessarily trigger their fight-or-flight responses. My surmise is that most Jews are deeply ambivalent about being "white." Very few of them take any pride in that particular phenotypical status.

By contrast, the second through line in Blacks and Jews dialogue, the subject of Israel/Palestine, does elicit fight-or-flight responses from Jews. Ferocious debates about the Israeli-Palestinian conflict and by extension the legitimacy of the Jewish state have characterized Black-Jewish interaction for more than half a century. The subject threads its way into countless intergroup conversations, even those at a remove from foreign policy concerns. Letty Pogrebin, in a classic 1982 essay, bemoaned a feminist conference she attended in which Black delegates supported a "Palestinian agenda item" in return for a plank of their own.[136] For decades, Jewish students on college campuses have reported feeling blindsided by the vehemence of anti-Israel criticisms made by their Black colleagues.[137]

With the exception of the radical Left, Jews across the political spectrum are likely to treat these sorts of criticisms of Israel as an existential threat to their *own* safety in the Diaspora. It marks a discursive space beyond their capacity for self-criticism. Many (but not all) Blacks, for their part, see the Jewish American defense of, or silence about, Israel's treatment of Palestinians in a negative light.[138] To them it indicates a lack of sensitivity to the plight of people of color who are confronted by overwhelming state power.[139] The conversation around this issue has devolved, often enough, into denunciations and/or disengagement and represents yet another arena in which Blacks and Jews dialogue breaks down.

It wasn't always this way. As Cornel West once put it, "Marcus Garvey was a Zionist. Du Bois was a Zionist. King was a Zionist."[140] Prior to the final years of the 1960s, Black civil rights groups were supportive of Israel. In so doing, they were in step with the majority of rank-and-file African Americans.[141] In the 1950s and the early 1960s, African American views toward Israel were generally positive.[142] The MBOs and the MJOs worked together, with the former offering a helping hand on Israel-based issues. A case in point: the NAACP lobbied to secure the votes of Haiti and Liberia in the historic vote of the United Nations (UN) on the partition of Palestine.[143] It was a different time; after all, it was a period where Jewish groups defended the Nation of Islam in court cases about religious freedom![144]

All of this changed in the final years of the 1960s, even as Martin Luther King consistently defended Israel from African American critics. Clayborne Carson has made the arch observation that tensions *within* the Black or Jewish community often exacerbated tensions between them.[145] Such was the case when younger, more radical activists challenged King's long-standing position of leadership in Black America.[146] When Stokely Carmichael and the Student Nonviolent Coordinating Committee unspooled their relentless anti-Israel rhetoric after the 1967 Six-Day War, they had many reasons for doing so. It wasn't only because of a growing interest in international affairs among Black intellectuals.[147] It wasn't only because everything from the 1955 Bandung Conference to the 1956 Suez Canal Crisis had sharpened their burgeoning critique of imperialism, colonialism, and global racism.[148] In addition, their anti-Israel approach was a signal to the Old Guard of a willingness to break with the liberal civil rights paradigm.[149] Carson's point thus provides a handy and subtle rule of thumb: Sometimes internal rifts *within* the Black and Jewish worlds spill over into encounters between Blacks and Jews.

In any case, the intervention of Stokely Carmichael and other Black Power figures would fundamentally change the Black-Jewish dialogue until the present day and likely well beyond.[150] Among a younger generation of African Americans, the generally supportive, albeit measured, pro-Israel stances of the MBOs at the mid-twentieth century were gone; they were replaced by strident rhetoric and a "comradely identification with Palestinians and Arabs."[151]

The new narrative explicitly identified Israel as a Western, colonialist enterprise, treating Palestinians the way the United States did Blacks. And if the United States was white, then so was Israel. Here is Carmichael in a 1968 speech: "Our ally cannot be Israel; it must be the Arabs. You have to understand that, but you don't understand it because you don't think it's important. It is important because the so-called State of Israel was set up by white people who took it from the Arabs."[152]

The embrace of the Palestinian and Arab cause by a generation of Black Power activists dismayed liberal and center-left Jews.[153] The sheer vehemence of the critique led many to reassess their role in the Grand Alliance and to turn inward. Earlier, I asked when the Blacks and Jews' relationship began. Since many have argued that the relationship is essentially finished—an opinion I do not share—it may be interesting to mention what event(s) symbolized its collapse.

The rise of the Black Power movement and the "purges" of the Jewish Left from the Student Nonviolent Coordinating Committee are oft-cited turning points.[154] On the heels of that came the Ocean Hill–Brownsville teachers' strikes, a conflict that turned all of New York City into a sound stage upon which Blacks and Jews could lob antisemitic and racist provocations at one another through the mass media.[155] Still other commentators, such as J. J. Goldberg, have urged readers not to underestimate how much damage the Jewish neo-conservative critique of affirmative action did in the 1970s.[156] All are possible inflection points, especially if we concede that the relationship had fault lines from the start. But since we are looking at foreign policy, we should note that the so-called Andrew Young affair did not help either.[157]

On July 26, 1979, US ambassador to the United Nations Andrew Young, an accomplished diplomat and the future mayor of Atlanta, undertook an apparently unauthorized meeting with Zehdi Terzi, the UN observer of the Palestine Liberation Organization (PLO).[158] The encounter took place in the New York apartment of Kuwait's permanent representative to the UN Abdullah Bishara.[159] The Israeli intelligence agency, the Mossad, learned of the get together and helpfully leaked the details to *Newsweek* magazine.[160] Predictably, a firestorm ensued. Young's meeting trespassed upon former secretary of state Henry Kissinger's mantra from his days in the Nixon and Ford administrations that there would be "no negotiations with the PLO until it recognizes UN Resolution 242 and the right of Israel to exist."[161] The Jewish community, reeling from a decade of PLO terrorist attacks on soldiers and civilians, decried the meeting. On August 15, Young promptly resigned, or in the opinion of some, he was forced to resign.[162]

Young is a figure of great stature among African Americans, and his resignation outraged many in the community. In an emergency meeting convened at the NAACP headquarters, the two hundred or so prominent Black leaders in attendance collectively issued a statement that decried "the inherent arrogance in the attacks on Ambassador Young by certain Jewish groups."[163] The statement continued, "Jewish organizations and intellectuals abruptly became apologists for the racial status quo."[164] These critics also did not look away from Israel's diplomatic relations with the apartheid state of South Africa, yet another flashpoint in the Blacks and Jews drama.[165]

In the present day, whatever movement there is in Black and Jewish dialogue about Israel/Palestine is a movement apart. The key agent would be the Black Lives Matter movement, whose intellectual DNA is much closer to that of Black Power thinkers than it is to the civil rights leaders of the mid-twentieth century. BLM emerged after the 2013 acquittal of George Zimmerman for the murder of Trayvon Martin in 2012, and the movement gathered steam after Michael Brown's murder in Ferguson, Missouri, in 2014.[166] The outrage over the killing of yet another Black man by police coincided with the latest chapter of the Israeli-Palestinian saga; for as protestors demonstrated in Missouri, the Israeli army had entered Gaza in retaliation for rocket fire.[167]

A 2015 video titled *When I See Them, I See Us* tightened the connections between certain sectors of the Black and Palestinian activist communities.[168] Featuring intellectual luminaries such as Cornel West, Alice Walker, and Angela Davis, among others, the three-minute video linked police brutality against Blacks in the United States with the killing of Palestinian children in the 2014 Gaza incursion. The effort to twin US law enforcement with the Israeli army results in passages such as this one: "They burned me alive in Jerusalem. They gunned me down in Chicago. They shot our water tanks in Hebron. They cut off our water in Detroit. . . . They sterilize us without our knowledge."[169]

By 2016 the Movement for Blacks Lives released a policy brief that touched on Middle Eastern affairs.[170] Its arguments were not likely to build bridges with Jewish American voters. Linking domestic and foreign policy priorities, it argued that resources necessary for "reparations and for building a just and equitable society domestically" have been funneled overseas.[171] Thus, aid to Israel made the United States complicit in a "genocide taking place against the Palestinian people," one carried out by an "apartheid state."[172] These proclamations were rounded out with a call for divestment.[173]

Reactions among the Jewish Right have gone precisely as one would expect.[174] Among the much larger American Jewish Center and Left, however, the BLM platform created considerable sadness and feelings of despair.[175] On the one hand, they hope for the removal of a right-wing government in Israel that has ruled for decades on end. In so doing, they cling to the belief that Israel is a democracy, one that can course correct and pursue a just peace with Palestinians. On the other hand, they are in near-total lockstep with BLM's political objectives, save its views on Israel. Rabbi Jonah Pesner of Reform Judaism's Religious Action Center noted that of the forty positions in the BLM statement, he wholeheartedly agreed with almost all of them.[176]

The invocation of words such as "genocide" and "apartheid," and strategies such as divestment, will make dialogue between BLM supporters and liberal and progressive Jews difficult. Difficult but not impossible. For one, these Jews continue to support BLM; if anything, their allyship was strengthened in the aftermath of the murder of George Floyd.[177] Second, they recognize that BLM's positions on Israel might not be pervasive in the entire Black community or even closely held by all members of a movement of such size. Still, alongside recriminations about antisemitism and racism, no dialogue in Blacks and Jews is more fraught than this one.

Conclusion: *Blacks and Jews

If we are to use the shorthand "Blacks and Jews," it must be accompanied by an asterisk that reads: *Jewish Americans are both Black and White and all things in between.* That truism cuts in all sorts of ways for the old, non-asterisked cast of participants in Blacks and Jews dialogue. By that I mean the recognition of Jewish diversity upends many previous staples of this discussion. Blacks, to paraphrase Baldwin, need not hate Jews anymore because they're white, while white Jews might be enjoined to think a lot more carefully about systemic racism as something that impacts members of their *own* community. White Jews celebrating Passover, as Lewis Gordon points out, might reflect on slavery in the United States, not just in ancient Egypt; BLM activists, at the very least, could recognize that the majority of Israel's Jewish citizens are people of color; and so forth.

Still, a defect of *Blacks and Jews, like its predecessor, is that it inti-
mates some sort of community-wide engagement, as if *all* African
Americans (approximately 47.8 million people) and *all* Jewish Americans (about 7.5 million people) were having a dialogue, or an argument, or a relationship.[178] Even in the so-called golden era of the 1940s
and 1950s, this was not the case, nor was it at any point in their engagement. Small subsets of Jews and Blacks have had relationships (think
of the MJOs and the MBOs), or relationships linked to dialogues (think
of the conversations between women, as noted earlier), or patterned
encounters (think of the messy, tense day-to-day interactions in the
big cities).

If Black-Jewish engagements have historically occurred between
very sociologically specific groups of individuals, I wonder if a more
self-conscious application of this practice constitutes the way forward.
During this turbulent period in the history of the United States, let
those who are similar seek one another out and converse among themselves. The immediate future of *Black and Jews, then, lies in affinity
groups. My surmise is that lesbian, gay, bisexual, transgender, and queer
(LGBTQ) persons in each community can find common ground. Members of the ultra-Orthodox Chabad movement could plausibly see eye
to eye with their equally God-fearing, and anti-secular, Black counterparts in the Pentecostal Assemblies of the World. The same might hold
for anti-Zionists and Israel supporters. The former can read Stokely
Carmichael speeches together aloud and invite anti-Zionist Jews to
give impassioned speeches. The latter can hold conferences about Ba-
yard Rustin's group Black Americans in Support of Israel Committee
(BASIC, founded in 1975) hosted in the American Israel Public Affairs
Committee's headquarters in Washington, DC.[179]

Thus, the Harold Cruse Principle is taken to its logical ends! Whether
seeking dialogue solely with those who will likely agree with you is a
cultural best practice, or a temporary solution to a complex problem,
or the end of civilization as we know it is something I will leave for
another commentator. But if this chapter demonstrates anything, it is
this: To have meaningful relationships, affinity groups must have equality. If there is one goal that *all* *Blacks and Jews dialogues should strive

for, it is that of creating structural equality for African Americans. Let that be the starting point of these dialogues.

I wish to close by suggesting that *dialogue* is only one, and not the most fundamental, component of the Black-Jewish encounter. I wonder if what most Blacks and Jews have done together in the far-flung West is something different, something that occurs at a level deeper than dialogue; that is, *Blacks and Jews, and not just subsets of these people, have always *looked at one another very carefully*. Observing—that is the missing verb in the catchall phrase.[180]

The examples of the two groups' eyeing one another could be multiplied at will. "The Jewish journey has had special implications for the black journey," wrote John Gibbs St. Clair Drake.[181] Indeed, throughout African American history, Blacks have looked at Jews for models of their own path forward. Booker T. Washington urged his people "to imitate the Jew."[182] Marcus Garvey was fascinated by Zionism, as were so many other Pan-Africanists.[183] Barbara Smith recalls the admiration in her uncle's voice as he often declared, "When they didn't let 'the Jew' in somewhere, he went and built his own."[184] Blacks, many Blacks, watch Jews.

Jews, for their part, looked to African Americans in a variety of ways. Scholars have argued that Jews who partnered with Blacks in the early twentieth century were not in it solely for brotherhood.[185] They knew full well that what happened to Blacks on Tuesday might happen to white Jews on Wednesday.[186] Recent research also suggests that Jewish Americans were deeply influenced by the Black Power movement. According to Marc Dollinger, the Jews copied the movement's unapologetic inward turn. With the fierce rhetoric of Black nationalism in mind, Jews felt compelled to ask aloud, "Is it good for the Jews?" Writes Dollinger, "By watching Black Power advocates press for greater African American empowerment, Jews learned how to reinvigorate their own ethno-religious community."[187] Jews, many Jews, watch Blacks.

*Blacks and Jews are perfervid observers of one another. Voyeurs, for sure. Exhibitionists, perhaps. If that is the case, then the next sequence of questions concerns *why* they fix their gaze so steadfastly upon one another. The affinity is in the observance. The observance is the affinity. Nothing suggests that they will stop doing that any time soon.

Notes

1. Chireau and Deutsch, "Introduction," in Chireau and Deutsch, *Black Zion*, 6.

2. Ms. Garza "grew up as Alicia Schwartz, . . . raised by her African-American mother and Jewish stepfather." See Cobb, "Matter of Black Lives." Garza also discussed her Jewish identity in a Facebook post: Garza, "Asking My Jewish Friends." For the complicated question of the number of Black Jews in the United States, see Wolfson, "African American Jews," in Chireau and Deutsch, *Black Zion*.

3. The key texts about Jews being accorded the racial status of white are Brodkin, *How Jews Became White Folks*; and Goldstein, *Price of Whiteness*, 217.

4. Newton, *Facing Black and Jew*, 10.

5. For some accounts, see Greenberg, *Troubling the Waters*, 213; Weiss, "Long-Distance Runners," in Salzman and West, *Struggles in the Promised Land*; Rose, "Blacks and Jews," 55–69; Friedman, *What Went Wrong?*, 202–3; Goldberg, *Jewish Power*, 24; and Dollinger, *Black Power, Jewish Politics*, 28.

6. On this fear, see Berlinerblau, *Campus Confidential*. There is, or was, a Center for Afro-Jewish Studies at Temple University founded by Professor Lewis Gordon, though it studied Afro-Jews as opposed to the traditional relations of Blacks and Jews. The center is discussed in D. Michaels, "Temple Professor Works to Create Center on Afro-Jewish History," *Jewish Exponent*, June 14, 2013, https://www.jewishexponent.com/2013/06/14/temple-professor-works-to-create-center-on-afro-jewish-history/. Also see Gordon, "Afro-Jewish Ethics?," in Hutt, Kim, and Lerner, *Jewish Religious and Philosophical Ethics*, 216.

7. Adderly, *Fiddler on the Roof*; Paley, "Zagrowsky Tells," in *Collected Stories*; Katz, *Don Byron*; Malamud, *The Tenants*; Beatty, *Tuff*; and Walker, *Meridian*.

8. Charles Mills offers the most comprehensive rundown of the ways in which Blacks and Jews are similar and different. See Mills, "Dark Ontologies," in Kneller and Axinn, *Autonomy and Community*. Also exploring this same-yet-different issue is Lester, "Lives People Live," in Berman, *Blacks and Jews*.

9. See Shapiro, *Crown Heights*; John Kifner, "Death on 125th Street: The Overview; Gunman and 7 Others Die in Blaze at Harlem Store," *New York Times*, December 9, 1995, https://www.nytimes.com/1995/12/09/nyregion/death-125th-street-overview-gunman-7-others-die-blaze-harlem-store.html;

and Malcolm Gladwell and Nancy Reckler, "8 Die after Gunman Sets Fire in Harlem," *Washington Post*, December 9, 1995, https://www.washingtonpost.com/archive/politics/1995/12/09/8-die-after-gunman-sets-fire-in-harlem/03c89590-139e-4013-8631-67397807f433/. For more on Freddy's, see Lee, *Civility in the City*, 2–3. Friedman, *Jews and the American Slave Trade*, 242, also points to instances of violence against Jews in Philadelphia between 1968 and 1972.

10. Shapiro, "Charleston Shooting"; BBC News, "Charleston Church Shooting"; Bowman, Saldivia, and Van Sant, "Suspect Charged"; and Winter, Romero, and Smith, "How a Deadly Shooting Unfolded."

11. Also espousing the principle is Greenberg, *Troubling the Waters*, 8. On the complexity of the relationship, see Berson, *Negroes and the Jews*, 9; and Holden, "Reflections," in Washington, *Jews in Black Perspectives*, 183.

12. Carson, "Politics of Relations," in Berman, *Blacks and Jews*, 131.

13. Jonas, *Freedom's Sword*, 8. On Jewish members of the start-up NAACP, see Greenberg, *Troubling the Waters*, 24; Perry and White, "Post–Civil Rights Transformation"; Rose, "Blacks and Jews"; and Lewis, "Parallels and Divergences."

14. On the Grand Alliance, see Salzman, "Struggles in the Promised Land," in Salzman and West, *Struggles in the Promised Land*, 1; and Glazer, "Jews and Blacks," in Washington, *Jews in Black Perspectives*. On the grand coalition, see St. Clair Drake, "African Diaspora," in Washington, 22.

15. Greenberg, *Troubling the Waters*, 114.

16. Dismissing concerns that Jews were self-interested (and blaming them on "revisionist historians") and stressing the ideological affinity of Jews for Blacks is Murray Friedman in *What Went Wrong?* Seth Forman claims that Jewish "vulnerability" throughout the Diaspora "imbued Jews with a more conscious recognition that the values of . . . civic liberty are matters of paramount concern." See Forman, "Unbearable Whiteness," 123. The argument is further developed by Forman in *Blacks in the Jewish Mind*.

17. Diner, *In the Almost Promised Land*, xv, xvii; Diner, "Drawn Together by Self-Interest," in Franklin et al., *African Americans and Jews*; Greenberg, *Troubling the Waters*, 43; and Weiss, "Long-Distance Runners," 123.

18. At a 1959 Nation of Islam meeting in New York, Malcolm X claimed that the Jew "is one of the worst devils. He does more to take advantage of the so-called black man than any other and yet poses as being a friend." See Anti-Defamation League, *Malcolm X*; Franklin, "Portrayal of Jews," in Franklin et al., *African Americans and Jews*; and Cruse, *Crisis of the Negro Intellectual*, 260–61. Cruse, though, was speaking more about Black-Jewish encounters in the Communist Party and the entertainment industry.

19. For example, Black figures such as R. L. Vann of the *Pittsburgh Courier* expressed considerable dissatisfaction and skepticism when J. E. Spingarn, a Jew, assumed the presidency of a Black organization in 1930. See Harrison-Kahan, "Scholars and Knights."

20. See Friedman, *Jews and the American Slave Trade*.

21. In a 1990 interview with the *Washington Post*, Farrakhan alleged that "certainly . . . some Jews were responsible on the ships that brought our fathers to slavery." See Louis Farrakhan, "Excerpts of Interview with Louis Farrakhan," *Washington Post*, March 1, 1990, https://www.washingtonpost.com /archive/politics/1990/03/01/excerpts-of-interview-with-louis-farrakhan /3dd71dd3-bce2-42ea-bd65-78cb3511ddal/; and Louis Farrakhan, "Farrakhan on Race, Politics, and the News Media," *New York Times*, April 17, 1984, https:// www.nytimes.com/1984/04/17/us/farrakhan-on-race-politics-and-the-news -media.html.

22. Farrakhan, "Minister Louis Farrakhan's Letter"; and Friedman, *Jews and the American Slave Trade*, 3.

23. The Nation of Islam's Historical Research Department, *Secret Relationship*.

24. Sundquist, *Strangers in the Land*, 3.

25. See, for example, Martin, *Jewish Onslaught*, 130. On Afrocentric views, see Berlinerblau, *Heresy in the University*.

26. Drescher, "Jews and New Christians," in Sarna and Medelsohn, *Jews and the Civil War*, 67.

27. Drescher, 67–69. As Drescher observes, many of the Jews involved in the slave trade were the descendants of those who had been forcibly Christianized in 1497. These "New Christians" were prominent in the slave trade, though Drescher argues there is no reason to consider them to be Jews.

28. Davis, "Jews in the Slave Trade," in Salzman and West, *Struggles in the Promised Land*, 66.

29. Korn, "Jews and Negro Slavery," in Dinnerstein and Palsson, *Jews in the South*, 91–96. Eugene Bender surmised that "one fourth of Southern Jewish adults were slave owners." See Bender, "Reflections on Negro-Jewish Relationships," 60.

30. Silverman, "Law of the Land," in Salzman and West, *Struggles in the Promised Land*, 74.

31. Silverman, 75.

32. Rosen, "Jewish Confederates," in Sarna and Mendelsohn, *Jews and the Civil War*, 228.

33. Korn, "Jews and Negro Slavery," in Dinnerstein and Palsson, *Jews in the South*, 130; and Silverman, "Law of the Land," 76.

34. Korn, 133; and Greenberg, "Becoming Southern," 62.

35. Kaplan, "Judah Philip Benjamin," in Dinnerstein and Palsson, *Jews in the South*.

36. Cited in Friedman, *What Went Wrong?*, 22.

37. Morgan, "Eugenia Levy Phillips," in Sarna and Mendelsohn, *Jews and the Civil War*, 272.

38. On Jewish abolitionists in the South, see Sokolow, "Revolution and Reform," in Sarna and Mendelsohn, *Jews and the Civil War*. See also Ruchames, "Abolitionists and the Jews," in Sarna and Mendelsohn; and Greenberg, *Troubling the Waters*, 15. On manumission societies, see Bender, "Reflections on Negro-Jewish Relationships," 59.

39. Webb, *Fight against Fear*, 218.

40. In 1876 Pinckney B. S. Pinchback said the following about the Jews: "Like you they were once slaves . . . and after they were emancipated they were met with persecutions." It is hard to tell if he is speaking about biblical Israelites or aforetime Jews. See Shankman, *Ambivalent Friends*, 115.

41. In all likelihood, earlier descriptions will be found in African American newspapers and slave narratives. See Gardiner et al., "Future of the Negro."

42. Some early instances from the 1890s are discussed in Hellwig, "Black Images of Jews," in Adams and Bracey, *Strangers and Neighbors*. He also shares Black views on Jews from 1885 and 1890; see Hellwig, 301.

43. Lewis, "Shortcuts to the Mainstream," in Washington, *Jews in Black Perspectives*, 85.

44. Reed, "Blacks and Jews," in Adams and Bracey, *Strangers and Neighbors*, 731.

45. See Weiss, "Long-Distance Runners," 127.

46. Lewis, "Shortcuts to the Mainstream," in Washington, *Jews in Black Perspectives*, 90. Also see Carson, "Politics of Relations," 136.

47. On the cities, see Gutman, "Parallels in the Urban Experience," in Washington. Also see Diner, "Between Words and Deeds"; Kaufman, "Blacks and Jews," in Salzman and West, *Struggles in the Promised Land*; and Trotter, "African Americans, Jews," in Franklin et al., *African Americans and Jews*.

48. Sobel and Sobel, "Negroes and Jews," in Rose, *Ghetto and Beyond*, 401. Making the same point is Himmelfarb, "Negroes, Jews, and Muzhiks," in Rose, 416. Also see Kaufmann, "Thou Shalt Surely Rebuke," in Hentoff, *Black Anti-Semitism*.

49. Sobel and Sobel, 385. That Jewish peddlers and merchants in the South also exhibited this tendency to engage with Blacks has been noted. Cheryl Greenberg has pointed out that in the North (and South), Jews "were more willing than most white Americans to serve Black clients and maintain stores in Black communities." See Greenberg, "'I'm Not White,'" in Sicher, *Race, Color, Identity*, 40. On the pattern in the 1960s, see Levine and Harmon, *Death of an American Jewish Community*.

50. Goldstein, *Price of Whiteness*, 53.

51. Shankman, *Ambivalent Friends*. Contra an 1881 complaint about Jewish vendors who discriminated in New Orleans, see p. 123.

52. Key texts here are Cruse's *Crisis of the Negro Intellectual* and, in the fictional register, Himes's *Lonely Crusade*. See also Buhle and Kelley, "Allies of a Different Sort," in Salzman and West, *Struggles in the Promised Land*.

53. Carson, "Blacks and Jews," in Adams and Bracey, *Strangers and Neighbors*, 576.

54. This was as true of the North as it was of the South, where the Jewish record on civil rights is far worse. Webb's *Fight against Fear* is a melancholy ode to "the contribution of an embattled minority in the destruction of Jim Crow" (219). An excellent comparison of southern and northern Jews is offered by Dollinger, "'Hamans' and 'Torquemadas,'" in Bauman and Kalin, *Quiet Voices*; Goldstein, *Price of Whiteness*, 147; and Moore, "Separate Paths," in Salzman and West, *Struggles in the Promised Land*.

55. Diner, "Drawn Together by Self-Interest"; Diner, "Between Words and Deeds," 89; Goldstein, 1; and Kaye/Kantrowitz, *Colors of Jews*, 49.

56. Making this point well is Vorspan, "Blacks and Jews," in Hentoff, *Black Anti-Semitism*, 208–9. Also see Kaufman, "Blacks and Jews," 108–9.

57. hooks, "Keeping a Legacy," in Berman, *Blacks and Jews*, 232.

58. hooks, 232.

59. The works are Newton, *Facing Black and Jew*; Buddick, *Blacks and Jews*; and Goffman, *Imagining Each Other*. We might consider Sundquist's *Stranger in the Land* as a fourth example, seeing the great attention he pays to fiction.

60. The philosopher Jane Anna Gordon, for example, points to the blind spots in Hannah Arendt's analysis of American racism. Her critique identifies a glaring double standard. Arendt, Gordon argues, failed to apply her own philosophical and moral framework for thinking through Jewish suffering in Europe to that experienced by Blacks in the United States. Working within James Baldwin's paradigm, Gordon speaks of Jews' "hungry adoption of whiteness." See Gordon, "What Should Blacks Think?," 231.

61. Greenberg, *Troubling the Waters*, 22–23, 33–35, 77–78, 80, 94–95. On the National Council of Jewish Women, see Rogow, *Gone to Another Meeting*, 186–87; and Shankman, *Ambivalent Friends*, 125. Interestingly, one study I consulted did not indicate that Jewish women engaged in much activism with Black women. See Klapper, *Ballots, Babies, and Banners*.

62. Schultz, *Going South*, 2, 193. Of interest, but not discussing relationships with Jews, is Morris, *Womanpower Unlimited*.

63. On the effect of these dismissals for Black-Jewish relations, see Sundquist, *Strangers in the Land*, 315.

64. For documents on this, see Baker and Cooke, "Bronx Slave Market," in Adams and Bracey, *Strangers and Neighbors*; Gurock, *Jews of Harlem*, 184–87; and Goldstein, *Price of Whiteness*, 161.

65. Baker and Cooke, 373. The issue surfaced even in 1990 as Jewish students reported their first encounters with a Black person had often been with housekeepers. See Schoem and Stevenson, "Teaching Ethnic Identity," in Adams and Bracey, 831.

66. Pogrebin, "Ain't We Both Women?," in *Deborah, Golda and Me*, 281.

67. Pogrebin, 283.

68. Pogrebin, "Blacks, Jews, and Gender," in Salzman and West, *Struggles in the Promised Land*.

69. Pogrebin, 388.

70. Smith, "Between a Rock," in Adams and Bracey, *Strangers and Neighbors*, 765.

71. Smith, 766. Similar sentiments are expressed by hooks, "Keeping a Shared Legacy," in Berman, *Blacks and Jews*, 230.

72. Hentoff, *Black Anti-Semitism*.

73. A notable exception in the volume is Vorspan's "Blacks and Jews," in Hentoff.

74. See Harris, *Ocean Hill–Brownsville Conflict*; and Pritchett, *Brownsville, Brooklyn*.

75. Erica Chenoweth and Jeremy Pressman, "This Is What We Learned by Counting the Women's Marches," *Washington Post*, February 7, 2017, https://www.washingtonpost.com/news/monkey-cage/wp/2017/02/07/this-is-what-we-learned-by-counting-the-womens-marches/; and Tim Wallace and Alicia Parlapiano, "Crowd Scientists Say Women's March in Washington Had 3 Times as Many People as Trump's Inauguration," *New York Times*, January 22, 2017, https://www.nytimes.com/interactive/2017/01/22/us/politics/womens-march-trump-crowd-estimates.html.

76. Chenoweth and Pressman; and Pagano, "Women's March."

77. Farah Stockman, "Women's March Roiled by Accusations of Anti-Semitism," *New York Times*, December 23, 2018, https://www.nytimes.com/2018/12/23/us/womens-march-anti-semitism.html.

78. The witness to the remark was Evvie Harmon. See McSweeney and Siegel, "Is the Women's March?"; and Stockman.

79. To be clear, however, this particular incident occurred before the January 2017 Women's March. See Stockman.

80. McSweeney and Siegel, "Is the Women's March?"

81. Stockman, "Women's March"; and Petra Marquardt-Bigman, "The Feminist Farrakhan Fans Who Organized the Women's March," *Times of Israel*, May 14, 2017, https://blogs.timesofisrael.com/the-feminist-farrakhan-fans-who-organized-the-womens-march/.

82. A long-standing grievance of Jewish feminists has been the presence of antisemitism in the women's movement. See Pogrebin, "Anti-Semitism." Also commenting on these accusations is Smith, "Between a Rock," in Adams and Bracey, *Strangers and Neighbors*.

83. See Locke, *Black Anti-Semitism Controversy*.

84. Baldwin, "Negroes Are Anti-Semitic," in Berman, *Blacks and Jews*.

85. Baldwin, 35.

86. Baldwin, 37.

87. Baldwin, 39.

88. That Jews "opted" to become white is a position Jane Gordon finds in Baldwin's "On Being White. . . and Other Lies." See Gordon, "What Should Blacks Think?," 227.

89. Baldwin, "Negroes Are Anti-Semitic," in Berman, *Blacks and Jews*, 37.

90. Calling attention to a similar trope in Black criticism of Jews are Lerner and West in *Jews and Blacks: A Dialogue*.

91. Goldstein, *Price of Whiteness*, 125.

92. On eastern European Jews' rejecting white identity, see Gordon, "Afro-Jewish Ethics," in Hutt, Kim, and Lerner, *Jewish Religious and Philosophical Ethics*, 218.

93. Greenberg, "'I'm Not White,'" in Sicher, *Race, Color, Identity*, 42.

94. Brodkin, *How Jews Became White*.

95. Goldstein, *Price of Whiteness*, 128; and Buhle and Kelley, "Allies of a Different Sort," in Salzman and West, *Struggles in the Promised Land*, 207–8.

96. Cruse, "My Jewish Problem," in Hentoff, *Black Anti-Semitism*, 156.

97. Cited in Evans, *The Provincials*, 269. Evans was citing research by Gary Marx for the ADL.

98. Smith, "Between a Rock," in Adams and Bracey, *Strangers and Neighbors*, 770.

99. Smith, 771–72.

100. Greenebaum, "Placing Jewish Women," 52.

101. Willis, "Myth of the Powerful Jew," in Berman, *Blacks and Jews*, 196.

102. Bellow, *Mr. Sammler's Planet*, 34.

103. See Goldstein, *Price of Whiteness*, 51, 62. Goldstein also points out that eastern European Jews tended not to see themselves as white, 76.

104. hooks, "Keeping a Shared Legacy," in Berman, *Blacks and Jews*, 230.

105. Crenshaw, "Demarginalizing the Intersection," 140.

106. Carbin and Edenheim, "Intersectional Turn."

107. Crenshaw, "Demarginalizing the Intersection," 140.

108. Greenebaum, "Placing Jewish Women," 51, 43; and Beck, "Politics of Jewish Invisibility," 95–96. Then again, the definition of intersectionality has further expanded over the years to include a more diverse set of social and political identities. See sociologist Collins's "Intersectionality's Definitional Dilemmas," 2. Crenshaw herself has reworked and broadened her definition from her original 1989 paper. See African American Policy Forum's interview, "Kimberlé Crenshaw."

109. Schraub, "White Jews," 382. Berkovits notes that by placing Jews into the "white" category, intersectional theory "downgrad[es] the significance of anti-Semitism." See Berkovitz, "Critical Whiteness Studies," 86.

110. Haynes, *Soul of Judaism*, 2.

111. Parfitt, *Black Jews in Africa*; Bruder, *Black Jews of Africa*; Landing, *Black Judaism*; Chireau and Deutsch, *Black Zion*; Azoulay, *Black, Jewish, and Interracial*; Gordon, "Rarely Kosher"; Gordon, "Réflexions sur la question"; Gordon and Dayan-Herzbrun, "Pourquoi les juifs"; Gordon and Alcoff, "Philosophical Account"; Kaye/Kantrowitz, *Colors of Jews*; Sicher, *Race, Color, Identity*; Bruder and Parfitt, *African Zion*; and Tobin, Tobin, and Rubin, *In Every Tongue*.

112. Gordon, "Review of Falguni A. Sheth," 123.

113. A similar taxonomy is given in Benor, "Black and Jewish," 52.

114. The term "civil rights babies" was coined by the demographer Barry Kosmin and mentioned in Wolfson, "African American Jews," in Chireau and Deutsch, *Black Zion*, 39.

115. Landing, *Black Judaism*, 10.

116. Fernheimer, *Stepping into Zion*, 5.

117. Landing, *Black Judaism*; Gold, "Black Jews of Harlem"; Brotz, *Black Jews of Harlem*; Gurock, *Jews of Harlem*, 174–76; and Haynes, *Soul of Judaism*.

118. On the Caribbean, see the remarks of Gordon and Alcoff, "Philosophical Account"; and those of Brotz, "Negro 'Jews,'" 325, 326, 329; Landes, "Negro Jews in Harlem," 179; and Landing, 13.

119. Brotz, 335, talks about Rabbi Wentworth Arthur Matthew and other Black Jews' negative perceptions of white Jews. Also see Landes, 175, 183.

120. For the general sentiment of white Jews as impostors, see, for example, Ben-Jochannan, *We the Black Jews*.

121. Fernheimer, *Stepping into Zion*, 12.

122. Fernheimer, 12–13.

123. Dorman, "'I Saw You Disappear,'" 62; Brotz, "Negro 'Jews'"; and Landes, "Negro Jews in Harlem." Also see Landing, *Black Judaism*, 137–40.

124. Jackson, *Thin Description*. Also see Singer, "Symbolic Identity Formation," in Chireau and Deutsch, *Black Zion*; and Michaeli, "Another Exodus," in Chireau and Deutsch.

125. Michael Gold and Ali Watkins, "Suspect in Jersey City Linked to Afro Hebrew Israelite Group," *New York Times*, December 11, 2019, https://www.nytimes.com/2019/12/11/nyregion/jersey-city-shooting.html.

126. Haynes, "People of God"; Leslau, *Falasha Anthology*; Nash Onolemhemhen and Gessesse, *Black Jews of Ethiopia*; Lenhoff, *Black Jews*; and Ojanuga, "Ethiopian Jewish Experience."

127. See Bruder, *Black Jews of Africa*; and Bruder and Parfitt, *African Zion*. Some members of many of the Afro-Jewish groups mentioned in this paragraph may have migrated to the United States; that is why I mention them here.

128. See the figures cited in Wolfson, "African American Jews," in Chireau and Deutsch, *Black Zion*, 38; and Benor, "Black and Jewish," 53, offers estimates, based on various criteria, ranging from 90,000 to 270,000 people. Zev Chafets, in a piece on Rabbi Capers Funnye (whom we will meet later), placed the number at roughly 2 percent of the Jewish American population. See Zev Chafets, "Obama's Rabbi," *New York Times*, April 2, 2009, https://www.nytimes.com/2009/04/05/magazine/05rabbi-t.html. Additionally, a report put together by researchers from Stanford University and the University of San Francisco claimed that existing studies undercounted the population of Jews of color. In reality, the report concluded that Jews of color likely make up 12–15 percent of the American Jewish population. See Kelman, Tapper, Fonseca, and Saperstein, "Counting the Inconsistencies." The number of Afro-Jews

will vary greatly depending on whether we count self-professed Jews or only those who are Jewish according to normative Jewish law (Halacha) as decided by leading Jewish denominations in the United States. In 2000 while leaning on the National Jewish Population Survey of 1990, Bernard Wolfson mentioned the number 132,000 and quoted Rabbi Funnye to the effect that there were 250,000 Black Jews in the United States ("African-American Jews," 38, 52n6). For the most recent discussion, see Haynes, *Soul of Judaism*, 3.

129. Kelman, Tapper, Fonseca, and Saperstein.

130. Gordon and Dayan-Herzbrun, "Pourquoi les juifs," 102: "Aux yeux de beaucoup de juifs blancs, se présenter comme Afro-juif c'est donc avoir d'abord été chrétien. Les Afro-juifs (juives) font ainsi face à la délégitimation de leur histoire juive." (In the eyes of many white Jews, to call oneself an Afro-Jew means you were once a Christian. Afro-Jews [who are Jews] are thus confronted with the delegitimation of their Jewish past.)

131. Walker, *Black, White, and Jewish*, 25; and Haynes, "Member of the Club?," in Sicher, *Race, Color, Identity*.

132. Though not with Sephardic Jews, who Afro-Jews report treat them much more kindly. See Haynes, *Soul of Judaism*.

133. Rinn, "Black Jews."

134. Bruce Haynes discusses some of these efforts in *Soul of Judaism*, 1–27. See also Fernheimer, *Stepping into Zion*, 5.

135. Rinn, "Black Jews," 13. Funnye could be considered both a Black Jew and a black Jew since he is ordained in both traditions.

136. Pogrebin, "Anti-Semitism," 45.

137. Lerner and West, *Jews and Blacks: A Dialogue*, 143–44.

138. Gary Rubin makes the important point that even after the 1960s, Blacks' views on Israel were more nuanced, diverse, and supportive than some Jewish critics alleged. See Rubin, "African Americans and Israel," in Salzman and West, *Struggles in the Promised Land*. Also see Richard Sklar on how "ethnic logrolling" led Black congresspersons to vote in a pro-Israel direction in the 1980s: "Africa and the Middle East," in Washington, *Jews in Black Perspectives*, 144.

139. On this point see West, "On Black-Jewish Relations," in Berman, *Blacks and Jews*, 147; and Hill, "Black Zionism," in Franklin et al., *African Americans and Jews*.

140. Lerner and West, *Jews and Blacks: A Dialogue*, 109.

141. Weisbord and Stein, *Bittersweet Encounter*.

142. Raab, "American Blacks and Israel," in Wistrich, *Anti-Zionism and Anti-semitism*, 155. For polling data from the 1980s, see Rubin, "African Americans

and Israel," 363. On Martin Luther King's support of Israel, see Sundquist, *Strangers in the Land*, 109.

143. Weisbord and Kazarian, *Israel in the Black American Perspective*, 20.

144. Dollinger, *Black Power, Jewish Politics*, 29, 39.

145. Carson, "Blacks and Jews."

146. Sundquist, *Strangers in the Land*, 110.

147. Cruse suggested this interest was piqued by Italy's ill-fated Ethiopian adventure in the 1930s. See Cruse, "My Jewish Problem," 157–58.

148. Keith Feldman notes that "the 1956 Suez Crisis began to reveal the possibility of Afro-Arab culture- and class-based solidarities." Additionally, the crisis supposedly "clarified the pressing demands for Afro-Arab solidarity" and dampened the appeal of Afro-Zionism for Black intellectuals. See Feldman, *Shadow over Palestine*, 64. Moreover, according to Annalisa Jabaily, Black nationalists resonated strongly with "a growing international consciousness and maturing theory of global subordination and colonialism." They embraced the view that "Jewish nationalism was subordinating Palestinian nationalism" partially due to Israel's alliance with the colonial powers of Great Britain and France during the Suez Crisis. See Jabaily, "1967," 212–13. On the Bandung Conference, see Sundquist, *Strangers in the Land*, 153; and Lubin, *Geographies of Liberation*.

149. Carson, "Blacks and Jews," 583.

150. Sundquist, *Strangers in the Land*, 319.

151. Sundquist, 8.

152. Carmicheal, *Stokely Speaks*; and "Stokely Carmichael Contends Palestinian Arabs in Just Struggle against Israel," *Jewish Telegraphic Agency*, April 10, 1970, https://www.jta.org/1970/04/10/archive/stokely-carmichael-contends-palestinian-arabs-in-just-struggle-against-israel. On the connections between the anti-racist thought of black intellectuals and "decolonizing struggles across the globe," see Feldman, *Shadow over Palestine*, 62. Feldman cites SNCC spokesperson Ralph Featherstone as making the same associations as Carmichael, 72. Carmichael, who had grown up around radical Jewish activist circles, certainly knew how to push Jewish buttons. (In this regard, he resembled Professor Leonard Jeffries, another figure who trafficked in antisemitic rhetoric, though he had once been president of his Jewish college fraternity.) See Goldberg, *Jewish Power*, 327. Like the radicals, he grew up in the Bronx; his rhetoric was over the top and incendiary. Famously, Carmichael likened Israelis to Nazis in their treatment of Palestinians. Meanwhile, SNCC purged non-Blacks from their organizations—an event that some commentators point to as the cradle of identity politics. On SNCC's infamous newsletter, see Carson, *In Struggle*, 266–69.

153. See Michael Lerner's observations in Lerner and West, *Jews and Blacks: A Dialogue*, 86.

154. Buhle and Kelley, "Allies of a Different Sort," in Salzman and West, *Struggles in the Promised Land*, 214–17.

155. Kaufman, "Blacks and Jews," in Salzman and West, 116–17.

156. Goldberg, *Jewish Power*, 317; Glazer, "Jews and Blacks," in Washington, *Jews in Black Perspectives*; and Chanes, "Affirmative Action," in Salzman and West.

157. Friedman, "Intergroup Relations," 123; and Jones, *Flawed Triumphs*, 130.

158. In most standard accounts, the meeting was unauthorized, though some confusion lingers as to whether "State Department treachery" was involved; hence, the meeting had been authorized. Jones, 144.

159. Friedman, "Intergroup Relations," 123; and Jones, 132.

160. Walters, "Young Resignation," 7.

161. Terry, "Carter Administration," 153.

162. Jones, *Flawed Triumphs*, 132.

163. Quoted in Friedman, "Intergroup Relations," 125. On Young as "the fall guy," see Holden, "Reflections," in Washington, *Jews in Black Perspectives*.

164. Thomas Johnson, "Black Leaders Air Grievances on Jews," *New York Times*, August 23, 1979, https://www.nytimes.com/1979/08/23/archives/black-leaders-air-grievances-on-jews-backed-contact-with-plo.html; and Friedman, 124.

165. On the dissatisfaction in the Black community with Israeli support of South Africa, see St. Clair Drake, "African Diaspora," 23–26; and Chazan, "Fallacies of Pragmatism," in Washington, *Jews in Black Perspectives*.

166. Rickford, "Black Lives Matter," 35.

167. Isaacs, "How the Black Lives Matter."

168. The video was made by the Black-Palestinian Solidarity campaign in the United States. See Black-Palestinian Solidarity, "World: *When I See Them, I See Us*," *Washington Post*, October 14, 2015, https://www.washingtonpost.com/video/world/when-i-see-them-i-see-us/2015/10/15/c8f8aa40-72c2-11e5-ba14-318f8e87a2fc_video.html.

169. Black-Palestinian Solidarity. This sequence begins at 1:18 and ends at 1:56.

170. The Movement for Black Lives is "a collective of more than 50 organizations representing thousands of Black people from across the country." Movement for Black Lives, "Vision for Black Lives."

171. Movement for Black Lives, "Cut Military Expenditures Brief."

172. Movement for Black Lives. Also see Dollinger's discussion in *Black Power, Jewish Politics*, 187–91.

173. One of the coauthors, Rachel Gilmer, was an Afro-Jew, albeit one who moved away from Judaism. See "Rachel Gilmer," *The Forward*; and Debra Nussbaum Cohen, "The Jewish Activist behind the Black Lives Matter Platform Calling Israel's Treatment of Palestinians 'Genocide,'" *Haaretz*, September 8, 2016, https://www.haaretz.com/world-news/americas/.premium-the-jewish-activist-behind-the-black-lives-matter-platform-calling-israels-treatment-of-palestinians-genocide-1.5422310.

174. Days after the Movement for Black Lives released its 2016 platform, Jonathan Tobin expressed his concerns regarding "the Left" in *Commentary*. "At stake here is not just the fulminations of extremism," he wrote, "but also the growing normalization of anti-Semitic attitudes." See Tobin, "Anti-Israel Left," para. 2.

175. Isaacs, "Feeling Torn."

176. Julie Zauzmer, "Jewish Groups Decry Black Lives Matter Platform's View on Israel," *Washington Post*, August 5, 2016, https://www.washingtonpost.com/news/acts-of-faith/wp/2016/08/05/jewish-groups-decry-black-lives-matter-platforms-view-on-israel/; and Wexler, "American Jewish Groups." This agreement about everything but Israel was noticed in the 1960s as well. See Dollinger, *Black Power, Jewish Politics*, 161.

177. Emily Wax-Thibodeaux, "Young Hasidic Jews Protest in Support of Black Neighbors, Challenging History of Racial Tensions," *Washington Post*, June 19, 2020, https://www.washingtonpost.com/national/young-hasidic-jews-challenge-history-of-community-tensions-with-protest-in-support-of-black-neighbors/2020/06/19/e16aea56-abdf-11ea-a9d9-a81c1a491c52_story.html; Prusher, "This Is What"; and Schachner, Mayo, and Spilker, "Aleinu."

178. Tighe et. al., "American Jewish Population Project."

179. Weisbord and Kazarian, *Israel in the Black American Perspective*, 51.

180. I distinguish "observing" from Hasia Diner's important suggestion of each existing "for the other as a kind of mythic mirror." In her view, the groups used one another as a "cultural metaphor for the other." See Diner, "Between Words and Deeds," in Salzman and West, *Struggles in the Promised Land*, 88. As I see it, the act of observation is less freighted with assumptions about the other as metaphor and so forth. It's more of a reflex than anything else. The groups simply look at one another, starting from dozens of different premises and drawing an infinite number of conclusions.

181. St. Clair Drake, "African Diaspora," 21. For countless exhortations of this sort, see Shankman, *Ambivalent Friends*, 118.

182. Given COVID-19 restrictions, this text was accessed through the University of Macau. See Washington, *Future of the American Negro*, 47.

183. Hill, "Black Zionism."

184. Smith, "Between a Rock," 767.

185. Lewis, "Shortcuts to the Mainstream," 93.

186. This is not my line. I heard it at an Afrocentrism event in the 1990s, but I cannot remember who the speaker was.

187. Dollinger, *Black Power, Jewish Politics*, 15.

3

Liberalism and the Tragic Encounter between Blacks and White Jews

Terrence L. Johnson

... but they who wait for the Lord shall renew their strength;
they shall mount up with wings like eagles;
they shall run and not be weary;
they shall walk and not faint.

—Isaiah 40:31

I first encountered biblical Judaism at my grandmother's knee in a small Black Baptist church in northern Indiana.

Through song and preaching, I grew intimately acquainted each Sunday with the major prophets and characters from the Hebrew Bible. Moses, Esther, Elijah, and Deborah were as widely rehearsed as the names most commonly associated with the New Testament: Matthew, Paul, John, and Jesus. The preacher, deacons, and congregants seemed to embody the flesh of Moses and the children of Israel fleeing from bondage as they interpreted the Hebrew Bible through dance, tears, prayers, and clapping.[1] Their weeping eyes filled the Red Sea, I conjured in my imagination, when the preacher invoked Moses from the pulpit. Their belly-churning moans jammed my ears, signaling both the lingering dread of the past and the solace they formed in their creative responses to their own abandonment in the torturous wilderness of America.

The hundred or so congregants at Providence Baptist Church arrived in the North during the Great Migration, when women, men, and children fled horrific humanitarian injustices in the Jim Crow South.[2] My late grandmother Mrs. Mary Kate Johnson spent more than twenty years worshipping at Providence after she escaped the African American blood–filled Alabama soil where she was a sharecropper. She and fellow travelers carried in their heavy hearts Negro spirituals and indigenous folk beliefs and practices. Their wrinkled, worn hands remolded the traditions they learned in their rural birthplaces in Mississippi and Alabama to guide them to the nation's heartland, where they believed industrialization promised better jobs and a prosperous life.

Of all the songs, no other spiritual seemed to move my grandmother to tears and bodily twists as much as the song popularized by the late Aretha Franklin, "Oh Mary, Don't You Weep."[3] As a child, I didn't understand why the choir was singing a song to my grandmother Mary. I assumed it was trying to comfort her from the prior week's backbreaking work, generally six days of ten-hour shifts spent mopping floors and cleaning offices, bedrooms, and bathrooms at the state hospital for disabled and abandoned children and adults. The lyrics and the choir's adaptation of Aretha Franklin's moving rendition filled my grandmother with dignity and validated the unspoken suffering and grief that her children and friends ignored or chose not to see. "Oh, Mary, don't you weep." The line pierced my grandmother's heart whenever the soloist bellowed out the refrain. It made my grandmother Mary's eyes well up with tears. "Oh, Mary, don't you weep, don't you mourn . . . / Pharaoh's army got drownded, / Oh, Mary, don't you weep. / If I could I surely would; / Stand on the rock where Moses stood."

As the song wore on, my grandmother surrendered her body to the Spirit. For a few fleeting minutes, she and the biblical Mary were one. "God told Moses what to do. / To lead the Hebrew children through . . . / Oh Mary, don't you weep." Mary and Martha, according to sociologist Cheryl Townsend Gilkes (I learned as an adult), were exemplars of engaged and vocal women with immediate and direct access to Jesus. "The God that exists in the spirituals is a God who is both transcendently majestic and highly personal."[4] When I asked my grandmother why she loved the song, tears filled her eyes. She lowered her head and smiled. Without uttering a word, I knew her answer. The women mirrored the strength, the courage, and the fortitude she sought to embody. She found in them a biblical narrative she consumed daily as a strengthening prayer.

Weaving together the Exodus account of God's divine hand in history alongside the promise and arrival of God in the flesh (Jesus), the song opens with Mary weeping after her brother Lazarus's passing. The lyrics remind churchgoers of God's divine justice by taking them back to Egypt, where God ended their enslavement and freed the children of Israel; then the lyrics return churchgoers to the New Testament, where Jesus raised Lazarus from the dead.[5] The song captures a glimpse of God's promise to a community and is not necessarily paradigmatic of an impending liberation for everyone, especially African Americans.[6] Instead of seeking a promised land, my grandmother and churchgoers found in the narrative resources to expand their familial and personal possibilities in a world where she and her people were the damned of the earth.[7] The churchgoers' account of Exodus offers a new direction of imagining the future discussions of Blacks and (white) Jews in America, one based on retrieving the Exodus story as a tool for locating how Blacks and Jews might engage in politics, religion, and tradition.

According to US literature and culture scholar Eric J. Sundquist, Blacks and Jews in the early twentieth century galvanized around their respective histories of suffering, slavery, and the Holocaust as opposed to the Exodus.[8] This set the conditions for imagining politics and political solidarity in and through white supremacists' histories and worldviews as opposed to establishing alliances based on postcolonial Exodus themes of dispossession, displacement, and wilderness. The latter points to a radical worldview that coincides with Rabbi Abraham Heschel's retort in 1963 that pharaoh was not dead but alive in the United States and living through white supremacists.[9] Whether one is wealthy or poor, engaging politics through examining a people's displacement or wilderness wandering, for instance, opens the possibility for engaging politics and public policy based on a divine promise of freedom that is constant but shifting. This hermeneutical turn neither negates traditional Jewish interpretations of Exodus nor privileges African American scriptural interpretations. Instead, the Exodus developed in my grandmother's church displaces the narrative from the confines of any singular group and molds it into a hermeneutical tool for understanding what it means to be displaced, dispossessed, and living in the wilderness, uncertain of how God's promise of freedom and deliverance would unfold. The move here shifts the debate from legitimating a "chosen people" to discovering how to produce a *material* and *spiritual* freedom for all human beings who encounter an Exodus people.

Exodus and American Exceptionalism

Noted historian Albert J. Raboteau cites the Exodus narrative as the most important textual resource for understanding the religious genius of African Americans. No other biblical narrative captured the imagination of enslaved Africans and their descendants more than the Exodus story.[10] It singularly transformed early Black life in the United States, offering a discursive site for African Americans to construct a new religious imagination, radical textual hermeneutics, and emancipatory political visions during the nineteenth and twentieth centuries.[11] In fact, Black politics and African American religions, including non-Christian traditions such as African American Judaism, African-centered religions, and the Nation of Islam, cannot be properly understood without examining African American encounters with the Exodus story in particular and the Hebrew Bible in general.[12]

Whereas African Americans read Exodus as a mandate for their freedom from slavery, Puritans read the story as a justification for their right to claim the land and to enslave Africans to work and cultivate it. The story unfolded seamlessly for the Puritans. They were the new children of Israel in a promised land given to them by God. By far the most noted New Englander to capture the Puritan spirit of the narrative is John Winthrop, who called the land a "City upon a hill." Winthrop's proclamation set the stage for how future leaders would characterize American democracy.[13] No other nation, so this story of America goes, is better prepared to fulfill on Earth the divine promise made to the children of Israel. What American Puritans envisioned as the New Jerusalem has in subsequent generations been translated into grand narratives of the nation as the world's only superpower to guarantee liberty, equality, and individual rights to everyone within its borders.[14]

During this current historic moment when the Black Lives Matter movement is leading a nationwide (and global) protest against police killings of unarmed African American people, African Americans are dying from COVID-19 at three times the rate of white people, and antisemitic violence and rhetoric are soaring, the nation is at a tipping point. Twenty-five years following the publication of Michael Lerner and Cornel West's *Jews and Blacks: A Dialogue on Race, Religion, and Culture in America*, Blacks and Jews are once again the glaring subtext of the nation's political and economic crisis. In 1995 the fight was aimed at improving liberalism. Now the talk is all about liberalism's shortcomings and whether it works at all.

Contesting Liberalism

In the decades following some of the strictest criminal justice laws and welfare cutbacks in modern history, BLM and the African American Public Policy Forum, for instance, are calling for widespread transformation to improve the lives of African American and Latinx communities. BLM has also linked Black political struggles to the Palestinian human rights struggle, creating a transnational movement for justice and freedom for the disenfranchised. The target of its discontent is liberalism, which is widely regarded to be race and gender blind. Liberalism is lauded for protecting individual rights and promoting equal access under the law. In the mid-twentieth century, John Rawls translated the emphasis on individual rights and liberties into an *ideal* political theory called political liberalism.[15] Guided by a desire to achieve social cooperation, liberalism aims to achieve two principles: political rights and equal access to economic opportunity.

But those underlying abstract principles threaten the future of Black and Brown lives. I have argued elsewhere that political liberalism is ill-equipped to protect Black and Brown rights-bearing citizens unless it takes into account gender and the "moral problem of blackness," commitments used by state and non-state actors alike to justify political and economic subjugation.[16] In *The Souls of Black Folk*, W. E. B. Du Bois characterized the problem in the form of a question: "How does it feel to be a problem?" The question lifted the veil to the white world's "contempt" and disdain for Blackness and Black people.

Karl Marx's "On the Jewish Question" raises a similar vexing concern for Jews. While Jews have benefited financially and professionally from liberalism and liberal policies, they remain the target of hate crimes and xenophobia. Jewish Americans' support of Israel and its expanding settlements in the West Bank, rightly or wrongly, place them on a collision course with BLM's alliance with Palestinians. Stuck between a rock and a hard place, Jews possess significant power relative to the size of their population in the United States, but they remain threatened by their status as the radical other. How do we talk about rights and liberties without also confronting the cultural impediments preventing some from exercising their freedoms without fear of death or persecution? That no amount of rights, liberties, or money can eradicate the cultural norms that maintain antisemitism is a challenge the nation must face.

William Hart captures the concealed weaknesses of the liberal political project in his poignant analysis of Marx's essay. According to Hart, *liberalism* "is a formalism that conceals the substantive operations of power and privilege behind notions such as equal rights. In the liberal state, Christianity is disestablished, diverted of its formal privileges, but 'on the ground,' in civil society, its power is unchallenged."[17] More often than not, political liberalism's supposedly race- and gender-blind pursuit of liberty ignored religion's actual role in obstructing equality and equal access, perpetuating dehumanizing norms of difference, and cultivating violence against non-whites and non-Christians.[18]

The "Negro problem" and the "Jewish Question" loom large in the United States and its ongoing efforts to revive liberalism. Blacks and Jews at different moments in US history personify a racial narrative of negation, both as the negative abstraction from white Christian ideals and as liberalism's unencumbered political subject. They emerge from what Lewis R. Gordon calls a "Manichean manifestation": "That protorace had its origin in theological naturalism brings these contradictions to the fore. The world of theological naturalism was, after all, one in which the theological and the natural were inseparable. There was no supernatural in that world because the natural was what the deity produced. Thus, instead of the natural and the supernatural, primary distinctions in Western modernity, there was the natural and the unnatural."[19]

Gordon's argument translates into a peculiar racial psychology that has sustained itself in varying iterations since 1619. Blackness is the literal sign or embodiment of despair, despondency, and the unnatural. Based loosely on racial pseudoscience of Black inferiority, the nation established a legal system to determine property rights, citizenship, housing codes, and commerce. Despite sometimes-contradictory efforts, the legal system sustained the category of "the white" over the course of two hundred years by systematically and systemically denying Blacks access to political life and to equitable economic opportunities. Put differently, white power was expanded, and cemented in and through, the denial of Black rights and power. Now, as writers and scholars expose the legal and economic barriers whites put in place to sustain such Black oppression and subjugation, they increasingly expose whiteness for its symbolic and beneficial qualities. Gordon puts it this way: "Blackness unmasks the false security of whiteness."[20]

Liberalism creates this Manichean choice: White Jews then must choose whiteness or face a violent crucifixion. For African Americans, such a choice is not an option, for they have no authority that the legal system is compelled to respect. Whether one is middle class or poor, class status in most instances will not shield Blacks from police harassment or police violence. Theirs is a choice between freedom and unfreedom. In both instances, for Jews and Blacks alike, returning to the lingering problem of the Exodus story might create the conditions for solving their respective problems. Just as the nation confronts the living legacy of slavery, so, too, those in exile must answer the question Edward Said raised more than thirty years ago: "How can one exit Egypt for an already inhabited promised land . . . and call it 'liberation'?"[21]

Returning to Exodus

By returning to the archives of Black and (white) Jewish encounters, I hope that political theorists, activists, and artists might ponder newfound possibilities as well as the limits of imagining and remembering

history, historic wrongs, and origin stories for purposes of constructing emancipatory practices, beliefs, and traditions. As I explore in this
chapter, Blacks and (white) Jews mirror the savants Du Bois examined
in *The Souls of Black Folk*, pursuing a freedom that can be found only
through the soul.[22] The tragedy, however, is that they did not find
their souls as Du Bois had anticipated. Unlike my grandmother and
her peers during the Great Migration who recovered and reinterpreted
the Exodus story to deconstruct and decode their immediate circumstances, elite Blacks and Jews in too many instances ignored and took
for granted the epistemic and emancipatory value of the Exodus story
to help them achieve a new freedom and promised land.

Specifically, they failed to reckon with the mythic warning against
worshipping false idols such as political and economic power. They
bracketed the Exodus story and the faith in God exemplified by that
story and relied instead on a rights-based liberal philosophy to seek economic, cultural, and political safety, recognition, and power in America,
the surviving idols from the biblical narrative they equally and wholeheartedly embraced. At the heart of this choice is bad faith.[23] On the
one hand, bad faith materialized among Jewish immigrants when they
ignored, overlooked, or condoned white antisemitism in their ascension
to middle- and upper-middle-class America. On the other hand, accommodationist and integrationist political traditions symbolized the bad
faith operative among elite Blacks. In both instances, however, Blacks
and (white) Jews underestimated the "metalanguage of race" and the
way in which the "theodicean grammar of the world in which race
was constituted is also . . . one about the negation of life and death."[24]
As long as elite Blacks and Jews pursue a blind liberalism without acknowledging its link to empire, or pharaoh, they will continue to pay
a steep price—namely, the death of Blacks and Jews. Rabbi Heschel
suggested a similar fate awaited whites: "It is time for the white man
to strive for self-emancipation, to set himself free of bigotry" by confronting the founding texts that support racism and antisemitism. For
African Americans, one path toward emancipation can be found within
the Negro spirituals.

As regards the former, from the civil rights movement to the Black
Lives Matter movement, we see a varying but similar refrain among

African Americans, a refrain demanding rights, justice, and equity through public appeals, protests, boycotts, and legal action. As regards many white Jews, the land of Israel serves as a crucible for imagining the possibility of their freedom, for restoring their strength, and for shielding them from annihilation. In both cases, for the African Americans and the Jews, the establishment that has led and represented each group has avoided untangling itself from liberal aspirations of equality, liberty, and justice through exercising rights and equal access.[25] Gordon characterized these liberal dreams as expressions of bad faith, manifesting not only in desires for true equality to and with elite and middle-class *whites* but also in their anguish, hatred, and befuddled distrust of each other. As evidence for my claim surfaces, I proffer two critical and abiding debates about slavery and assimilation.

First, the American Jews' engagement with Exodus takes a different path than that taken by Blacks. What seems undeniable, given Jews' extraordinary success as immigrants, is that the United States is anything but an "iron furnace." Jews' appreciation for the United States, as compared with the experience in European Christendom, is well known.[26] For many Jews, America *is* the promised land, an assessment verified by their well-earned socioeconomic achievements.

The Jews' lofty ascent in the United States leads us to ask how they interpret the Exodus story, and, here, the disconnect with their Black compatriots is most obvious. For most Jews, the Exodus narrative has the sense of a closed, bygone story, something that happened a long time ago, something that needs to be memorialized. The experience of bondage and displacement is not painfully real but encased in amber.[27]

The factors that compel most Jews to retain this distance from the story are widespread. The security provided by the existence of Israel as a haven in the unlikely event of catastrophe, the "whitening" of Jewish Americans whereby they have achieved a (complex and uneasy) acceptance into the American racial mainstream, and the secular orientation of many Jews that inclines them to see biblical stories as works of art or myths but not prescriptive in any way—all are the cause and effect of tremendous prosperity and acceptance within a liberal social world.[28]

Yet there have always been Jewish voices that have questioned *ideal* readings of texts. Gordon wondered aloud why white Jews on Passover focus so much attention on ancient Egypt, when the iron furnace for Blacks, followed by Jim Crow, was just a generation away:

> I know that for me, the question of enslavement is not remote, and though I very much doubt it is otherwise for many other Afro-Jews from North America and the rest of the Americas, it is also clear that many of us live in a world that wants to us to forget the ancient enslavement of people to whom many Euro-Jews engaged in such rituals are not actually related while insisting on our forgetting recent enslavement of people to whom most Afro-Jews are actually such.[29]

The competing uses of Exodus make strange bedfellows. On the one hand, the Puritans embraced the Exodus story as theirs, using it to justify seizing land from indigenous Indians in the New World.[30] On the other hand, Blacks and American Jews found resources in the same story to affirm their respective theologies. When they all sought to lay claim to their rights, the conflicting interpretations of the story converged and collided. Whereas once whites had insisted that the promised land was designed exclusively for Christian and white property owners, through persistent agitation, war, and technological advancements, the promised land slowly opened its borders to include economic and ethnic diversity. Even then, it remained largely off-limits to African Americans.[31]

Visions in Exile

The truth is that the Exodus narrative posed a problem neither group had addressed. It exposed the contradictions of American exceptionalism and the profound limits of its political descendant, political liberalism. The competing interpretations of the story between Blacks and Jews led, unfortunately, to a common conclusion: Their group embodiment as (white) Jew or African American Christian, and therefore as encumbered political actors, foreclosed the possibility of their entry into public life. With few exceptions, Blacks and Jews are a reminder of the theological conundrum at the heart of this nation's origin story and its self-understanding of liberalism and democracy: The United States is a stolen land built in brick and mortar by what whites allege to be a subhuman and immoral people (Blacks) and is a land established at the height of its industrialization through antisemitism and neo-Nazi commitments, especially within elite public arenas such as higher education.[32] The combined appropriation of the labor and economic capital of Blacks and Jews produces a racial liberalism that ignores racial, religious, and gender subjugation even as it seeks an ideal pluralism.

When Jewish immigrants, for instance, attempted to articulate the political justifications for their solidarity with African Americans, they appealed to biblical enslavement and the Holocaust to support their stance. For "central to any explanation of American Jewish liberalism is the vulnerability of Jews in the Diaspora. That is, a unique history of persecution appears to have imbued Jews with a more conscious recognition that the values of individual freedom, political and religious liberty, and civic equality are matters of paramount concern, even more so perhaps than marginal economic gain."[33] This shared understanding of group suffering mobilized many elite (white) Jews to support African Americans, especially during the first half of the twentieth century.[34] From this engagement, a narrative of Jews as wholeheartedly committed to anti-Black racism emerged within popular culture. Yet Black political leftists challenged the truth of Jews' commitment to social justice in the late 1960s, claiming that Jewish immigrants bracketed their Jewish identity whenever threatened by political or economic conditions.

Slavery in the Americas, not Egypt

During the tipping point in Black and Jewish encounters, African Americans were increasingly exploring the African slave trade and Jewish involvement in it. African American studies scholar Harold Cruse, for instance, examined US slavery to demonstrate the complexity of Jewish communities and their historic participation in eradicating anti-Black racism. Cruse's biting and bombastic argument characterizes the general tone of the debate: "As regards the slavery issue, American Jews *as individuals* were no different from the other individual American whites: They were pro-slavery, anti-slavery, slave-owners, slave-traders, pro-Union, pro-Confederate, war profiteers, army officers, soldiers, spies, statesmen, opportunistic politicians or indifferent victims of intersectional strife of the Civil War."[35] His point is compelling. Similar to the majority of the gentile community during US slavery, Jewish communities embraced the existing rules of capitalism and its legal doctrines.

In response to Cruse and others, Jewish scholars emphasize that "a small fragment of the Jewish diaspora" in Europe and the Americas were "entwined" in the African slave trade.[36] Of those involved, historian Seymour Drescher suggests, most were not involved in the direct trafficking of human commodities but in "the transportation and processing of certain tropical commodities—sugar, diamonds and tropical wood."[37] Despite its low-level engagement, the debates on Jewish involvement in African enslavement reinforces Cruse's assertion that shared suffering does not immunize either group from harming the other or from participating in an alliance based on self-interested economic and political practices.

The situation was similar regarding assimilation. Despite that, neoconservative pundit Norman Podhoretz chided African Americans who criticized Jewish immigrants for assimilating into gentile culture.[38] Instead of criticizing Jews, Podhoretz retorted, African Americans should address the social and cultural issues underlying their own economic and political plight. Assimilation is the answer to the Negro's problem. Podhoretz asserts that the survival of African Americans depends upon the erasure of "color": "And that means not integration, it means assimilation, it means—let the brutal word come out—miscegenation."[39] The rise of the Black Power movement and its rejection of liberalism and assimilation reinforced his argument, Podhoretz believed.[40]

Cruse and Podhoretz wrote at a virulent political moment.[41] However, their arguments failed to understand the essence of Black Power's argument: Systemic white supremacy and structural power were what was oppressing Blacks. In two different accounts, Cruse and Podhoretz explored individual behavior at the expense of interrogating the social structures that inform, and heavily influence, individual and group cultural behavior, political commitments, and economic outcomes. They both simply ignored the dearth of political and economic power within their respective communities. Had Cruse and Podhoretz, for instance, examined the structural effects of race, gender, religion, and class on Blacks and (white) Jews, they would have focused more on the discourse and structures (or systems) that inform oppression and discrimination rather than investigate individual "bad" actors and "poor" decision making.[42] Neither Cruse nor Podhoretz explicitly references the Exodus story, but their concern underscores an attitude expressed broadly in African American biblical exegesis: The wilderness—in this case, the nation's Black ghettos—is designed to afflict and confound the captive. In other words, the shared though shifting experiences of white supremacy by Jews and African Americans is not by coincidence; their systemic oppression is by "democratic design." In variant ways, the Exodus narrative therefore informs our investigations and interpretations of the history of America, race, and religion.

Between Assimilation and Power:
An Enduring Divide

The point about systemic oppression is worth highlighting to contextualize the enduring asymmetry between Blacks and Jews. Whether they pursued similar goals, ambitions, and aspirations or not depended on pragmatic political and economic concerns. Their interests coalesced in the early twentieth century when elite Blacks and Jews joined forces to institutionalize their fight against legalized racial discrimination and segregation with the 1909 founding of the National Association of Colored People, one of the last vestiges of Black and Jewish alliances.[43] As political science scholar Adolph Reed Jr. observes, for example, the relationship was conceptually weak and destined to implode in light of the groups' shifting class and economic interests. "With the exception of the radical Left . . . the Jewish / Afro-American relationship has been determined through the mediation of elite-driven formal advocacy organizations such as the NAACP and National Urban League (NUL) on the one side and the American Jewish Congress, American Jewish Committee, and the Anti-Defamation League of B'nai B'rith on the other."[44]

The rise of the NAACP and the NUL, which dates back to 1910, together highlights the institutional relationships between Jews and

Blacks. Such relationships were born of overlapping political fears and concerns facing Blacks and Jews alike. However, Jews, according to Reed, engaged the interracial conversations from both sides, as either the ethnically other or the social insider, which relates to their outsize role in the professions. Over time, the doubleness of Jewish identity created internal conflicts in determining the best political strategies and desired outcomes for organizations like the NAACP. "The peculiarity of Jewishness as a status that is neither racial, nor national nor, for that matter, necessarily religious exonerates Jewish elites from the imperative of organizational interracialism in their own domain while demanding obeisance to it from black civil rights organizations, as in the case of the black power elaboration out of the civil rights movement."[45]

Jewish Assimilation

Even if they had overlapping concerns, from the beginning Blacks and (white) Jews actually started their journey toward emancipation on dissimilar terms. American slavery's afterlife materialized in new legal and economic setbacks, such as legally blocking Blacks from pursuing the financial and political benefits of capitalist society vis-à-vis home-ownership, entrepreneurship, and citizenship. By contrast, Jewish immigrants arrived on US shores with skills germane for an exploding industrial economy. Yet awaiting them with open arms were communities informed by a vicious culture of antisemitism, which seemed to follow wherever Jewish immigrants attempted to establish a new home and community. Others welcomed their skills but not their full humanity. Between 1880 and 1924, as Eric L. Goldstein writes in *The Price of Whiteness*, Jewish immigrants possessed "skills and came from professions that didn't send them to the farms but to urban areas where they worked largely in commerce."[46]

Despite these divergent cultural and economic starting points, Blacks and Jewish immigrants nonetheless embodied within American culture *the* existential problem facing the nation: In their different ways, they were all antithetical to, and aberrations of, the nation's self-representation of *whiteness*, Protestant Christianity, and American exceptionalism. Before the advent of the civil rights movements,

Black and Jewish immigrants therefore found themselves meandering in the nation's wastelands—its urban ghettos, or places translated biblically as the *new* wilderness—as fellow "strangers" in a land where, writes Eric Sundquist, they experienced "an intermixture of empathy, anxiety, and hostility."[47] Harold Cruse and Norman Podhoretz remind readers in autobiographical essays they penned in the 1950s and 1960s of the asymmetry between the groups.[48] Cruse and Podhoretz reject any characterization of a shared experience of racism or oppression between Blacks and Jewish immigrants. Instead, they wholeheartedly blame the other or the other's community for their predicament in the United States. Sundquist is far more generous in his interpretation of the wilderness experience. Blacks and (white) Jews, he writes, "experienced very different, if sometimes parallel, dynamics of exclusion and inclusion while 'dwelling with' the dominant white, gentile culture."[49]

Marked by such exploitation and enslavement, Blacks and (white) Jews in the first half of the twentieth century were therefore undoubtedly tragic characters within the emerging empire. They were always reconstituting themselves but were consistently rejected by the gentile elite establishment, and in different ways, both were struggling to achieve freedom. "The tragicomic character of the Black and Jewish experiences in modernity—coupled with a nagging moral conscience owing to undeniable histories, underdog status, and unusual slavery-to-freedom narratives in authoritative texts—haunts both groups."[50]

Scripture and the Politics of Race

Why is the failure to embrace the Exodus story by Blacks and (white) Jews such an omission? The Exodus story contains two important dimensions of central importance to the study of Blacks and (white) Jews: enslavement and empire. Certainly enslaved Africans focused heavily on God's role in freeing the children of Israel from bondage in Egypt, but the Exodus narrative also foreshadows debates on structural economic disenfranchisement and governmental abuse of power. To these issues they paid less attention.

If we want to understand the creative genius that African Americans employed to reclaim the Hebrew Bible and the US Constitution as liberating texts, we must return to the enslaved Africans' encounter with the Bible. One step to such ends would be to explore the hermeneutical shift within Black religion. By inserting themselves and their history into the text, many Blacks interpreted the Bible both as the word of God and as a historical document. By no means was this an effort to interpret scripture based on their whims and petty individual desires; instead, they read scripture as a text in and through which all could see themselves and imagine how God would work among them just as God had done in the narratives of the Bible.

As the New Testament scholar Allen Dwight Callahan writes, the enslaved were primarily introduced to the Bible during the Great Awakening of the 1740s. The movement's heavy emphasis on charismatic preaching and engagement with scripture likely played a role in how the enslaved imagined scripture. Against this backdrop, a new framework for interpreting, understanding, and appropriating the Bible emerged. This hermeneutical approach developed two important concepts worth noting here: the Bible as a talking book and God's universal call to liberate the enslaved.

The Bible is probably the single most important text among the enslaved, and it served as a reference point in political debates long after slavery ended. Callahan argues that the Bible is fundamental to understanding Black life, especially during slavery. He goes so far as to argue that the Bible is the "book of slavery's children."[51] Indeed, the enslaved people's approach to scripture was fundamentally at odds with the standard interpretations of Christian enslavers. Callahan argues that slaves imitated what they heard in white sermons, but they created a new theological and hermeneutical starting point appropriate for their context. The shift, in part, had everything to do with how they were introduced to the Bible. Most slaves studied the Bible through oral recitations and subsequently memorized scripture before they ever laid eyes on the text. "It was through the human voice, then, and not the printed page, that the Bible came to inhabit the slave's inner world."[52]

From this orientation, the enslaved embraced scripture differently. They read the Book as embodying living and ongoing narratives, not as settled, "written text[s] but as spoken word."[53] The talking Bible created the conditions for displacing static traditions in favor of creative individual and group engagement with the narratives of scripture. "African slaves and their descendants discerned something in the Bible that was neither at the center of their ancestral cultures nor in evidence in their hostile American home: a warrant for justice in this world."[54] The focus on justice as a theological mandate became the basis for much of their worldview and religious orientation.

Though the path toward justice started with the Bible, it also involved introducing a hermeneutical shift that inserted the enslaved persons into the text, and that positioned them to write themselves into the text. This shift was intentional and reflected an ingenuity emerging from traditions buried within the segregated worlds of the Jews and African Americans. As Vincent Wimbush reminds us, in the United States the Bible was retrieved in an effort to "persuade different publics of the wisdom of the course of integration, the acceptance of all human beings as part of the American experiment." How the enslaved persons read it not only challenged the existing interpretation of scripture but also provided a paradigm for imagining the Bible within and in tension with established church dogma and doctrine. The enslaved persons cultivated a hermeneutical tradition of reading the Bible as a living document. "The contribution of African American religious traditions to hermeneutical theory is its modeling of a radical and consistent adherence to the primacy of interpretation (determination) of everything, including religious texts, through (a particular) 'world.'"[55] The Bible within Black religion is thus a living embodiment of God's call and response to the people of God. For African American Christians, biblical narratives are a reminder of God's presence in history and a reinforcement of God's ongoing work for the living.

The Exodus story framed the moral vision that underscored the politics of respectability in the late nineteenth century. African American studies scholar Eddie S. Glaude Jr. in *Exodus! Religion, Race, and Nation in Early Nineteenth-Century Black America* builds upon Michael Walzer's *Exodus and Revolution*. In Glaude's account, the Exodus motif provides the political vocabulary and imagination to galvanize a people against white supremacy. He describes Exodus as setting the stage for three important moves: racial solidarity, sense of peoplehood, and nation. "Exodus history sustained hope and a sense of possibility in the face of insurmountable evil. The analogical uses of the story enabled a sense of agency and resistance in persistent moments of despair and disillusionment."[56]

Exodus without Jesus and the Black Church

Critical race theorists and secular humanists charge scholars with isolating their interpretations of the Exodus story and Moses to the nineteenth century. Twentieth-century writers, literary scholar Michael Lackey asserts, abandoned Moses—and Christianity, for that matter—for cultural criticism and socialism. He points to Richard Wright and Zora Neale Hurston's essays and short stories on Moses to expose a countertradition of the Exodus story. Lackey calls these thinkers "African American atheists" who claim that Moses is a "dictator" and horrible leader.[57] Moses inaugurates monotheism, which, Lackey suggests in agreement with Sigmund Freud, sets the conditions for the emergence of Western imperialism.

African American studies scholar Robert Gooding-Williams takes some issue with Glaude's characterization of Exodus as a guiding political principle, "for it is residually a form of political expressivism, a politics predicated on a prepolitical idea of 'the meaning of being black,' where that meaning is identified not with something 'deep-rooted,' but with 'common problems."[58] Gooding-Williams stands against this singular meaning of racial solidarity. He insists that "more and more, blacks will disagree about the existence, nature, and significance and scope of antiblack racism, and their disagreement will be complicated and intensified by conflicting, intragroup class interests and by disputes relating to such issues as black feminism, the legitimacy of homosexual unions, and the appropriateness of interracial intimacies."[59]

Lackey and Gooding-Williams raise critical insights into Exodus studies in Black religion and politics. I agree we must acknowledge the countertradition of the Exodus story among African American atheists and secular humanists. But as a political symbol, the Exodus story nonetheless played a vital role in the political imagination of African Americans. Three examples are worth noting. First, we should turn to Marcus Garvey's Universal Negro Improvement Association (1914), an organization designed to promote self-reliance through economic and political independence. Its focus on Africa is an attempt to lead Blacks from the wilderness to Canaan. The association's emphasis on the politics of respectability and on racial uplift as grounding elements for economic freedom resemble the moral and legal edicts expressed by Moses to the children of Israel.

Second, an unusual and highly contested example is the Nation of Islam. Elijah Muhammad's emphasis on dietary restrictions and his theory of freedom seem to lean heavily on the themes of wilderness, freedom, and independence.

Third, Rev. Albert Cleage Jr., the founder of the Black Nationalist Christian Church of the Shrine of the Black Madonna, invoked Exodus to justify Black protest and urban unrest.[60] He challenged the people to "commit to a civil religion," one rooted in a Black nation—not the American republic.[61] Cleage "challenged them to become their own pillar of fire. As a pillar, he promised them collective strength enough to carry a nation. As fire, they would not blend quietly into the world around them, but they would shine brightly against a nightscape of despair and dispel false hopes of integration."[62]

The countertraditions of Exodus in twentieth-century African American writings sometimes run parallel to the postcolonial criticism of the narrative. The work of postcolonial theorist and professor of literature Edward Said is an exemplary case study.[63] In his book review of Michael Walzer's *Exodus and Revolution*, Said rejects three fundamental claims that Walzer makes: The Exodus story is not Western, it offers an uncritical interpretation of the Israelites, and it avoids the question of "chosenness." In an exchange with Walzer, Said raises two principle criticisms: First, Western interpretations of the Exodus story fail to describe the complex relationship between the Israelites and pharaoh; the heavy emphasis on the former's bondage is "unintelligible" to Walzer. Second, a "secular" political philosophy should not be overly dependent on redemption.[64] Said criticizes Walzer's claim that Exodus is an exemplary liberation narrative, especially so from the context of modern-day Palestinians. He asks, "How can one exit Egypt for an already inhabited promised land, take that land over, exclude the natives from moral concerns . . . kill or drive them out, and call the whole thing 'liberation'?"[65] Said thus poses a serious challenge to the liberatory uses of Exodus. For every freed Israelite, there appears to be an unfree *other* in the promised land. Without the conquest of Canaan, there is no Israel.[66] For that matter, without European expansionism in the West, there is no United States.

Said's probing argument takes us back to the challenges Rabbi Heschel raised in 1963 as well as the implicit concerns underlying Negro spirituals. Exodus cannot be used to sustain a singular group's freedom; instead, its abiding message sits in two fundamental axioms: First, the permanence of enslavement and cruel government are constant features of human existence. Second, the human imagination possesses the ingenuity and perseverance to resist and fight against dehumanization and hegemony.

Imagining Exodus within the context of a survival theology, as suggested by womanist scholar Delores Williams, relocates the narrative from the realm of myth to a cultural-political context. For African Americans, the cultural-political context is framed by a literary theory of the talking book that assumes a dialogical relationship between the reader and the text. As Gilkes demonstrates in her compelling work "Go and Tell Mary and Martha," the Exodus story was not retold to find freedom; instead, it was a symbol of the freedom already constituted within the human body and imagination.

Emancipation: Now What?

The Exodus freedom established in African American religions took a back seat to the rights-based approach to justice that institutions such as the NAACP pursued. While Exodus motifs remained operative in debates on justice and freedom, the institutional leaders focused on a strategy that assumed equal rights and equality under the law would safeguard the Exodus freedom. To better understand the tension between the Exodus freedom and the rights-based approach, I want to explore three themes: Jewish philanthropy, NAACP leadership, and gender and domesticity. In these examples is the foundational issue at the center of Black and Jewish encounters—that is, the fundamental asymmetry in their coalition work. In most instances, Jews held the financial and economic power to determine the direction of political work. In these cases, Jewish assimilation and successful appropriations of capitalism blinded them to liberalism's unavoidable anti-Blackness. Failing to realize the living pharaohs in America, elite Jews found it nearly impossible to "see" and empathize with African Americans' criticisms of capitalism, liberalism, and Jewish assimilation. This was a heavy load to bear for *both* groups. And this load was carried into the civil rights movement and the Black Power struggle, where the unaddressed problem or debate imploded.

For many Jewish businessmen, such as Sears, Roebuck and Company chief executive officer Julius Rosenwald, the history of antisemitism informed their philanthropic giving to African Americans. Historian Hasia Diner notes that Rosenwald was concerned with what he saw as a rebirth of Jewish oppression within the bodies of African Americans.[67] He joined forces with educator and Tuskegee Institute founder Booker T. Washington to fund primary and secondary public education for African Americans in the South. Washington's focus on Black self-help, entrepreneurship, and industry made him an ideal partner to alleviate Rosenwald's concerns of Jewish apathy toward the race problem. He and Washington contributed equally to fund more than five thousand schools in the South. Filmmaker Aviva Kempner, producer of the noted 2015 documentary *Rosenwald*, notes how the men's relationship played an indelible role in paving the way for the US Supreme Court's decision to end legalized school desegregation in *Brown v. Board of Education* (1954) and to establish the pathway for Blacks to enter the middle class.

The NAACP is well known for its integrationist model of leadership as it related to Black and Jewish male leadership in particular. A simmering but unaddressed problem was the balance of authority between the highly educated Black leaders and the wealthy Jewish benefactors and the Black leaders' criticisms of Booker T. Washington's accommodationist theory. Eric Goldstein claims that "wealthy Jews contributed to black causes to deflect attention away from themselves and to support black causes that emphasized Negro improvement."[68] Whatever motivated Jews—and I am sure they had many reasons—throughout most of the NAACP's early history, Blacks and Jews seemed to broker the power dynamics respectfully. However, the board of the NAACP imploded when Joel Spingarn was elected chair in 1930, inciting an unexpected internal revolt. James Weldon Johnson resigned as secretary of the board. As Du Bois describes in an unpublished essay, the moment created a buzz in and outside the organization.[69] "The NAACP argued that the ravages of capitalism without the benefits of democracy and human rights would be so exploitative that people of color would be unable to find any sense of justice and hope in their societies, moderate nationalist influences would be discredited, political extremism would take root, and the end result would be more violence, more deprivation, and more human rights violations."[70]

The tension between elite Blacks and American Jews surfaced as well in the encounters between Black women and white Jewish women. This relationship between Black women and Jewish women is a rarely discussed subject. The untold narrative stems, in part, from their asymmetrical relationship. Historically, the two groups most often engaged in domestic situations, with Black women serving as caretakers, nannies, and house cleaners for Jewish women and their families. In 1935 Ella Baker and Marvel Cooke captured the racial and sexual exploitation of Black women and their bodies.[71] In an assessment of their study, Joy James wrote: "Institutional sexism, racism, and segregation rendered black female employment synonymous to menial labor" in a society that "largely defined black women's work as domestic service for whites" and, in this instance, for Jewish women in particular.[72] Black women were also exploited by employment agencies. "As evident in its inadequate provisions for relief, the government shared much of the public's deep indifference towards black women trapped in domestic/sexual labor."[73]

Noted Black feminist Barbara Smith takes a more realistic tone when addressing gender in Black and Jewish encounters: "The love-hate dynamic not only manifests itself politically, when our groups have functioned as both allies and adversaries, but also characterizes the more daily realm of face-to-face interactions. I think that women of color and Jewish women sometimes find each other more 'familiar' than either of our groups find Christian majority W.A.S.P.s."[74]

In all three examples, the collision between racial capitalism, power, and anti-Blackness underscores the latent tensions between and the dissimilar plights facing Blacks and Jews. Eric Goldstein describes it aptly: Jews are consistently the other in American society, but unlike African Americans, who are repeatedly marginalized, Jews have not been marginal within structures of power and dominance in the United States. Unlike many immigrants, Jews arriving between 1880 and 1924 "had skills and came from professions that didn't send them to the farms but to urban areas where they worked largely in commerce."[75] Goldstein also observes that the vast majority of white Jews were in the middle class well before the eve of the civil rights movement: "In many ways, Jewish middle-classness was just the kind of success story Americans loved to hear and tell about themselves. Jews helped create American lore about boundless opportunity and individual pluck. American Jews living in new suburbs, full of new homes, new cars, and new consumer goods worked to prove that they could strengthen a middle-class American public and thus national interests."[76]

This success, however, was once again linked to American exceptionalism. Even when liberal Jews supported the civil rights platform, how they justified their support is striking. Goldstein shatters years of disputed history regarding white Jewish support of Black causes by arguing that starting in the 1950s, Jews rebuked anti-Blackness in light of liberal political principles—that is, liberty and voting rights—rather than grounding their social justice commitments in Jewish traditions such as the Exodus narrative.[77]

Goldstein's argument is compelling. Yet if, in fact, Jews by and large are invoking extensions of American exceptionalism and liberalism to advocate for racial justice, then the philosophical framework guiding them—the moral and political vision of liberalism as a fundamental home for Blacks and Jews—has a fundamental flaw: The racial and ethnic blindness that frames liberalism rejects or at least ignores the comprehensive nature of anti-Blackness and antisemitism.

Blacks and Jews Confront Liberalism

Long before Black Power signaled the end to political solidarity with or encounters between Blacks and Jews, the crumbling of their relationship started. It happened soon after the 1950s, when Jews were no longer considered a race but an ethnic group. The shift from a race—which presumed some solidarity or strong link to Blackness—to ethnicity initiated a shift in how whites perceived Jews. As an ethnicity, Jews were no longer solidly connected to Blacks. This initiated an upward climb toward assimilation for Jews that locked them into a category of racial *otherness*.

The NAACP's domestic agenda, meanwhile, was designed to reinforce one of the most influential theories of the late twentieth century—political liberalism.

Beyond Liberalism

Most scholars call upon Black Power in framing their discussion of the "rift" between Blacks and Jews, for Black Power's interest in nationalism, its criticism of Israel, and its anti-capitalist rhetoric alienated but also benefited Jews, according to Marc Dollinger. He claims Jews retrieved from Black Power a model by which to frame Jewish self-interests within the context of "identity politics." This was a major reversal. Dollinger writes that Jews joined the political struggles in the 1960s precisely to affirm their *whiteness* and *middle-class* status: "While Jews certainly claimed distinctive religious imperatives as their rationale for engagement, they entered political activism with a public affirmation that what was good for America was by definition good for the Jews. Support for civil rights meant that Jews understood what it meant to be American."[78]

Though Dollinger's argument is compelling, Cheryl Greenberg's argument is more convincing: Black Power not only illuminated the divergent political philosophies within Black politics but also crystallized the increasing schism between leftist Blacks and elite Jews. At issue during the late 1960s was a growing "loss of momentum in the struggle for justice. If there is a tragedy about the current dismissal it is that Americans have abandoned its noblest goals while leaving intact its deepest contradictions."[79]

On the one hand, Jews found in liberalism a system that partially rewarded the bracketing of one's racial or religious identity. It was not a matter of passing but of emulating gentile norms and habits. On the other hand, Blacks grew increasingly disheartened by the racialization of liberalism, with its limits on or impediments to Blacks' entry into elite spaces. They could imitate the dominant norms, as exemplified by the politics of respectability, but a biting reality persisted—the Negro problem. This created a growing dissatisfaction with liberalism as an achievable ideal. Criticisms such as the ones raised by Du Bois—that Blacks should attack the system itself for its economically exploitative nature—increasingly divided Blacks from Jews. I agree in part with Greenberg's explanation of this rift—that both groups grew tired of fighting for justice—but I would like to extend her argument: Justice is a failed project unless it aims to detangle justice from colonialism, egregious capitalism, and patriarchy.

The competing versions of justice emerged from simmering tensions as leftist Blacks rejected capitalism and liberal rights-based politics, and moderate and conservative Jews embraced Israel as a symbol and a formidable nation.

Unspeakable Questions

The 1967 Six-Day War expanded the Jewish Question into a global phenomenon, according to Harold Cruse.[80] In the United States, the war triggered fierce debate between Blacks and Jews during the emerging period of Black Power. Two key points surfaced from within the Black Power movement: Israel was an imperialist nation, and it was entangled in the apartheid so dominant in the Republic of South Africa. Stokely Carmichael and his followers saw the war as a symbol of Jews' growing domestic and global influence, which quickly diminished their immigrant status; indeed, they were no longer second-class citizens but people with land.[81] Israel's relationship with South Africa was ripe for criticism, especially among Black Power activists, many of whom had spent the previous decade or so building solidarity with those fighting against apartheid.

Scholars suggest that Israel's relationship with South Africa was pragmatic and necessary to solidify its sovereignty. Justified or not, says Naomi Chazan, it created enduring and harmful consequences. "In effect, Israel has appeared to relinquish the cause of liberation in South Africa at precisely the times as an international consensus has coalesced on the [obsolescence] of white domination in that area."[82] Chazan notes that Israel expressed clear and sharp opposition to apartheid during a meeting with the United Nations Human Rights Committee. Indeed, it had voted to censure South Africa in 1962, and by 1967 the countries' relations "had dwindled to a mere trickle."[83] Still, Israel's alliance with South Africa "furnished an all too convenient pretense for the expression of anti-Israeli sentiment."[84]

At the turn of the twentieth century, Jews imagined the Hebrew scripture as a reminder of enslavement and a historical origin story. When the enslaved Afro-Christians and their descendants inserted themselves into this Hebrew Exodus narrative, they integrated themselves into the treacherous and winding roads of transgressions and triumphs experienced by the children of Israel. As a guiding narrative, this Exodus story linked Blacks and Jews on a relentless journey to secure a homeland, one based loosely on nationalism and humanistic endeavors; that goal seemed to end with the Six-Day War. Whether justified or not, Israel's relationship with the United States and apartheid South Africa evoked immense distrust and disdain in Black leftist activists, many of whom saw these alliances as an acceptance of structural anti-Black racism at the expense of human rights.[85]

As the twentieth century unfolded, the increasing entrenchment of anti-Blackness and the evolving face of antisemitism created the conditions for an inevitable collision. The shifting and expanding category of whiteness, which allowed Jews, Italians, and the Irish to assimilate, cemented anti-Blackness into the nation's cultural, economic, and political structures. In so doing, it far outpaced the rise of antisemitism and other forms of ethnic discrimination. Eric Goldstein puts it this way: Jews remained a perennial other within elite contexts, even as they disproportionately occupied those spaces, but they were not marginalized. The marginalized, at least beginning with the birth of the civil rights movement, remained primarily Blacks, Hispanics, and some Asians.

Yet even as the experiences of oppression diverged and overlapped less and less, white supremacist practices forced the Blacks and (white) Jews to remain bedfellows. Antisemitism in fields such as business, law, and medicine meant that Black and urban areas were the primary places where Jews are allowed to serve. This translated into an invisible but real form of discrimination, which constructed Jews into the other; yet they were often regarded as a superior other, superior at least to Blacks. Hence, at the local, noninstitutional level, Blacks often experience Jews as the other and the "master," meaning that many Blacks are at some level aware of their inferior status to Jews. But as Baldwin reminded us in his 1967 *New York Times* op-ed, Blacks dismissed or rejected Jews' minority status because by and large the latter operate their businesses and practices as if they were white.

Baldwin's critical essay appeared around the birth of the Black Power movement, at a time when Blacks were demanding a radical transformation of American liberalism. Unlike Cruse's account of Black Power, which he insinuated was primarily rhetorical and aimed at reform, I believe the Black Power movement called for a fundamentally new vision of America, one that imagined democracy as a framework for pursuing global human rights and seeking freedom and liberation. This shift exposes two important points: the belief that Blacks would never achieve political freedom in America without robust power and the implicit cry for a homeland that is buried in the call for solidarity in what we now call the developing world. Blacks' embodied search for a homeland unfolded in the pursuit of new cultural expressions, the taking of new names for themselves—Stokely Carmichael became Kwame Ture—the birth of Kwanzaa by Maulana Karenga, and the call to emigrate to Africa.

Cultural nationalism and economic reform challenged some of the liberal norms that elite Jews employed when they supported Black liberal political struggles. Black Power's political agenda called for a swift overhaul of the distribution of political and economic power for Black communities. The movement's abrupt shift from individual reform to group reform and transformation alarmed many Jews. The liberalism they supported dates back to Franklin D. Roosevelt's New Deal. Unlike previous presidencies, Jews found a home in Roosevelt's administration, where they experienced "unprecedented access to the corridors of power" and influence. "Not only did many American Jews occupy prominent positions in the Roosevelt administration, but thousands more filled the rolls of local New Deal agencies, determined to leave an unmistakable Jewish imprint on the national landscape."[86] But the reform that allowed Jewish immigrants entry into the highest halls of power happened in large part due to their ability to assimilate and bracket their Jewish identities.

Black Power advocates decried Jews' emphasis on assimilation, as this move was impossible for the majority of African Americans (who could not pass as white).[87] To this end, Black political struggles in the late 1960s pushed for radical economic and political transformations that would lead to the possession of power, a diluted objective of the civil rights agenda of the King era.

The political strategy of Black Power's group-based political and economic agenda alarmed some Jewish groups. Unlike their enthusiasm for Roosevelt's New Deal, elite Jews found little excitement in President Lyndon B. Johnson's civil rights agenda. Indeed, when the "Great Society advocated group-based programs such as affirmative action, the Jewish community flinched. Establishment of rigid hiring quotas, which many Jews believed would be inevitable, was antithetical to Jewish interests. The Jewish community stood at a crossroads, wondering whether to follow the path to neo-conservatism along with many other ethnic groups or to embrace the new, more militant brand of liberalism."[88]

How do we come to terms with the tension between the politics of transformation as opposed to integration? Did they both fundamentally lose in their fight against white supremacy and legalized discrimination? In both instances, Black Power advocates as well as moderate and conservative elite Jews, respectively, paid a heavy price for rejecting and embracing liberalism.

For Black Power advocates, their denunciation of capitalism meant the federal government increasingly criticized and surveilled them, eroding their movement in metaphorical and tangible ways. Scholars must also wonder whether the movement's commitment to transatlantic alliances and human rights idealism created (unforeseen) parallel ideological problems that had plagued the Talented Tenth. David Levering Lewis's astute analysis of the Talented Tenth's aspirational pursuits of social and political leadership at the expense of seeking micro-level entrepreneurship within urban communities and ghettos is worth considering. The Pulitzer Prize–winning historian writes that the Talented Tenth focused far more on liberal philosophy, social acceptance, and the tragic sense of life rather than on entrepreneurship and economic power. "Racial aristocrats, steeped in classical education, . . . missed the significance of the butcher and tailor shops, the liquor stores and the pawnshops. They overstressed psychological and social, at the expense of economic and political solutions to race problems."[89] Lewis's argument is poignant and forceful.[90]

In these separate and yet overlapping pursuits of Blacks and Jews, I wonder if we see their sacrifice as examples of the price of fighting for and against a growing empire. In fact, the political uses of Black and Jewish bodies coincide with the increasing reliance of the federal government on American exceptionalism to justify its political and economic reach around the globe.[91] At one level, the nation's overt reliance upon exceptionalism as justification for that reach reinvents and reinserts into the conversation a politicized Christian notion of redemption; that is, the barbarians of the world—meaning this time Muslims, Hindus, and so on—must be redeemed by America's blood. We galvanize support for this by showing the Western world, and especially Americans, the barbaric doctrines and actions of the other, who must be punished for violating American or Western norms. Yet the blood that is sacrificed—or conjured up as irredeemable in twentieth-century America—is often that of Blacks, while Jews are more likely to be targets of random hate crimes and to be identified by hate groups as the enemy that must be destroyed. Systemic violence by state and non-state actors against Blacks and the perennial threat of persecution against Jews symbolize the price of American exceptionalism. (White) Jews symbolize the promise of American success; they are the darling of the immigrant narrative. Blacks are a reminder of what happens when people fail to assimilate and pay the price of a group's interior deficiencies. Blacks are perceived as problems that must be detained, disciplined, and (eventually) destroyed. By contrast, the blood of Jews symbolizes the price for occupying seats next to the pharaohs of power; they are assimilated but remain the perennial other, in exile (to reference Sundquist). This liminal state pierces Jews' souls while they pursue positions of power.

Conclusion

The congregants in my late grandmother's church might offer an answer to the liberalisms that bound together elite Blacks and (white) Jews. Both groups imagined the United States and the varying versions of its democratic ideals as a symbol of home, maybe not of the promised land but close to it. This is where they misinterpreted or misused one of their cherished traditions, the Exodus story. Police shootings of unarmed African American men and women, sentencing disparities in the criminal justice system, and Palestinian disenfranchisement, to name a few, are compelling both communities to reassess their historic aspirations to belong to the middle class and their acquiescence to *whiteness* as normative and superior.

In a piercing editorial in 2015, Rabbi Gil Steinlauf charged Jews to give up their whiteness if they want to fight racism. "I write about racism and Jewish identity not because we are not good people. I write about this because in recognizing race as central in American Jewish identity, we cannot only more effectively use our success in this country for good purposes, but we can return truly to the essence of what being Jewish in the world really means."[92]

Maybe we've all mishandled and misread the Exodus story, retrieving it to justify middle-class aspirations and blindly accepting liberalism as the only route to emancipation. This seems to be the case among Black and Jewish institutions such as the NAACP and the Jewish Federation. The spirit of the Exodus story informed the exceptional rhetoric of liberalism. It also established the cultural grounds for the uncritical and blind acceptance of American hegemony as normal and normative within the liberal tradition. The Hebrew story actually underscored an enduring, contentious, and perplexing bond between Blacks and white Jews long before they encountered each other in the United States. What bound them together happened long before their joint efforts to democratize America through liberalism and their liberal aspirations of justice and equality.[93]

Their unabashed belief in the Hebrew Bible as a formative epistemic tool to establish a collective understanding of justice, community, and

God's mythological role in human history characterized a connection that, on the one hand, would link elite Blacks and Jews during the civil rights movement and, on the other hand, would tear asunder the connections between leftist Black Power activists and increasingly middle-class and conservative American Jews after the 1967 Six-Day Arab-Israeli War.

What actually cemented the divide between Blacks and Jews remains contested. What is uncontested is that the elders, especially those whose hands formed and framed the traditional civil rights platform during the 1960s, want to revive those historic partnerships. By contrast, those who are reluctant to engage in this conversation are college-educated Blacks and many in the BLM movement.

Blacks and (white) Jews seem to be separated by mountains. In the era of BLM, socialist criticism of capitalism and the Palestinians' conditions in Israel will likely impede any meaningful conversations between Blacks and (white) Jews. Blacks' antisemitism and African Americans' support of figures such as Alice Walker and Minister Louis Farrakhan, both of whom are the face of antisemitism in many white Jewish communities, will likely prevent many (white) Jews from entertaining a renewed dialogue with African Americans.

The answer may be found by returning to the Exodus as living text. "Perhaps it is the will of God that among the Josephs [former slaves] of the future there will be many who have once been slaves and whose skin is dark. The great spiritual resources of the Negroes, their capacity for joy, their quiet nobility, their attachment to the Bible, their power of worship and enthusiasm, may prove a blessing to all mankind."[94] Buried somewhere in the spirituals and among a people whose dogged strength alone preserved their humanity, we may find the imagination to create a new vision. I recall a classic Negro spiritual, "Come and Go with Me to that Land," chanted in my late grandmother's church:

> Come and go with me to that land
> Come and go with me to that land
> Come and go with me to that land
> Where I'm bound
> Where I'm bound

I got a brother in that land . . .
I got a mother in that land . . .
I got a father in that land . . .

Where I'm bound
Where I'm bound

The future is unknown. But on the journey—in the struggle to protect
and sustain human flourishing against oppression—sits the promise
bound to a land where peoplehood is dismantled, borders removed,
and political struggles birth and sustain the art, music, and literature
needed to produce life.

Notes

1. African American abolitionists such as Maria W. Stewart are well known
for appropriating parts of the Exodus story to justify the eradication of African enslavement. To explore Stewart's prominent speeches, please see Stewart, *Maria W. Stewart*, 56–59. Kenyatta R. Gilbert's *A Pursued Justice* offers a
compelling analysis of the varying ways the Exodus story appears in Black
preaching. During the Great Migration, Black preachers returned to the narrative to provide additional assurance that God remained with them as their
congregants settled into their new homes (Gilbert, 3–4).

2. See Wilkerson, *Warmth of Other Suns*. She provides a rich account of the
political and moral aspirations of African Americans during the Great Migration.

3. According to Gilbert, "The Great Black Exodus had indeed signaled a
crucial turning point for African Americans. The complex matrix of dilemma,
promise, and opportunity had not only transformed an African American
'agrarian peasantry into diversified urban proletariat,' but it also aroused radical changes to worship practices and infrastructural operations" in many Black
churches (*Pursued Justice*, 23).

4. Gilkes, "'Go and Tell Mary and Martha,'" 567–68.

5. For a gripping autobiographical account of Franklin's rendition of "Oh,
Mary Don't You Weep," see Kenan's "Good Ship Jesus," 712–13. He writes that
he was "instantly bewitched by [Franklin's] version [of] a song older than the
Civil War, what historians call a slave song" within the tradition of Negro
spirituals (712).

6. Williams, *Sisters in the Wilderness*, 133. I agree with Williams. The Exodus account is not "paradigmatic" of Black liberation. Instead, she suggests that readers envision it as a *holistic story* rather than a single event. This would open the readers' eyes to the messy and complicated notion of liberation within the Hebrew Bible. Indeed, not everyone is liberated by God.

7. Here, I am referencing Fanon's *Wretched of the Earth*. Lewis R. Gordon translates Fanon's text as *The Damned of the Earth*. Gordon writes in *What Fanon Said* that the "damned" refers to harm or injury upon Blacks by way of their negation as nonliving beings.

8. Sundquist, *Strangers in the Land*, 92.

9. Heschel, "Religion and Race."

10. Raboteau, *Fire in the Bones*, 28.

11. Raboteau, 27–28. Along with Raboteau's groundbreaking work, a number of scholarly books have contributed to deepening the public's understanding of the Exodus story within Black religion and politics. Such texts include Glaude, *Exodus!*; Marbury, *Pillars of Cloud and Fire*; Maffly-Kipp, *Setting down the Sacred Past*; and Patterson, *Exodus Politics*.

12. For additional information on the reach of Exodus in African American religions and Black nationalist traditions as well, please see Redkey, *Black Exodus*.

13. Rogers M. Smith makes the case that US president George W. Bush invoked Winthrop's characterization to affirm America's religious identity and its distinct "democratic faith." Please see Smith, "Religious Rhetoric," 284.

14. Please see Miller, "Errand into the Wilderness."

15. I go into more detail on Rawls and race in my essay "On the Limits of Rights and Reason."

16. Johnson, "On the Limits."

17. Hart, *Edward Said*, 145.

18. Nicole Flores has a book forthcoming on the topic regarding religious violence and politics titled *The Aesthetics of Solidarity*.

19. Gordon, "Race, Theodicy," 727.

20. Gordon, 730.

21. Walzer and Said, "An Exchange," 253.

22. Du Bois, "Of Our Spiritual Strivings."

23. I borrow Lewis R. Gordon's definition of *bad faith*, which is reflective of the conditions that force subjects to project their self-interests or ideal beliefs in (for instance) liberty and equality at the expense of truth of the lived experience of Blackness. See Gordon, *Bad Faith and Antiblack Racism*.

24. Higginbotham, "African American Women's History," 253–54; and Gordon, "Race, Theodicy," 725.

25. The Blacks Lives Matter movement might be the one exception.

26. For additional information of the uses of Exodus within social movements, please see Walzer's *Exodus and Revolution*.

27. Alvin Rosenfeld notes that as early as 1897 some Jews identified the United States as "our Zion." He writes that "Zion was a precious possession of the past . . . but it is not our hope of the future. America is our Zion. Here, in the home of religious liberty, we have aided in founding this new Zion." Rosenfeld and Davis, "Promised Land(s)," 115.

28. Rosenfeld and Davis, 122–23.

29. Gordon, "Afro-Jewish Ethics?," in Hutt, Kim, and Lerner, *Jewish Religious and Philosophical Ethics*, chap. 11.

30. For a critical examination of the jeremiad and its role in anti-Black racism, please see Shulman, *American Prophecy*.

31. Hebrew Bible scholar Jon Levenson takes a slightly different view. He sees a sharp difference in how Blacks and Jews utilize Exodus. Black liberation theology's reading is especially focused on demonstrating God's active hand in history and God's willingness to stand alongside the poor and oppressed. Levinson sees very little historical evidence to support the Exodus narrative as a real historical event. He challenges readers to come to terms with biblical traditions that condoned enslavement and promoted what contemporary readers would interpret as injustice.

32. Several scholars have noted that President Donald Trump's racist behavior is tied to the country's long history of racism, xenophobia, and sexism. In "Donald Trump," Henry A. Giroux writes that recent protests and blatant attacks against Blacks and immigrants stem from "a discourse that betrays dark and treacherous secrets about the state of American culture and politics" (32).

33. Forman, "Unbearable Whiteness," 123.

34. Julian Bond notes that the shared experiences of discrimination "made the black-Jewish alliance inevitable and necessary, and Jewish support for black causes—for democracy's causes—absolute." Please see Bond, introduction, in Adams and Bracey, *Strangers and Neighbors*, 4.

35. Cruse, *Crisis of the Negro Intellectual*, 478.

36. Drescher, "Role of Jews," in Adams and Bracey, *Strangers and Neighbors*, 105–6.

37. Drescher, 111. He goes on to assert that both groups were distorted by the economic and political circumstances of the time. Indeed, Africans and

Jews "constituted two contemporary cohorts of people driven from their habitations at about the same moment in world history" (113).

38. Podhoretz, "My Negro Problem," in Berman, *Blacks and Jews*, 89–90.

39. Podhoretz, 91.

40. Podhoretz, 95. He slams what he calls "black-nationalist passions by the ideology of reverse discrimination" that he not only links to affirmative action but also to "demands that districts be gerrymandered to ensure the election of black legislators; and the next step seems to be government coercion to ensure that these black legislators will be 'authentic' and representative of the interest of Black Power" (95).

41. For a rich account of the conditions that led to Black Power, please see Carson's *In Struggle*.

42. Reed's essay, "Blacks and Jews," in Adams and Bracey, *Strangers and Neighbors*, played an important role in the development of this section. He notes that Blacks and Jews alike attacked structural discrimination in housing and higher education (734). However, both groups fought for integration rather than the whole-scale reformation of the preexisting norms and structural divides that created and sustained systemic racism.

43. Lewis, "Parallels and Divergences," in Adams and Bracey, 332. Lewis notes the NAACP relied on Jews to assist with fundraising and its administration (338).

44. Reed, "Blacks and Jews," in Adams and Bracey, 729.

45. Reed, 730.

46. Goldstein, *Price of Whiteness*, 36.

47. Sundquist, *Strangers in the Land*, 3–4.

48. Cruse, "My Jewish Problem," in Hentoff, *Black Anti-Semitism*; and Podhoretz, "My Negro Problem," in Berman, *Blacks and Jews*.

49. Sundquist, *Strangers in the Land*, 4.

50. Lerner and West, *Jews and Blacks: Healing*, 2.

51. Callahan, *Talking Book*, xi.

52. Callahan, 12.

53. Callahan, 2.

54. Callahan, xiv.

55. Wimbush, "Reading Texts through Worlds," 139.

56. Glaude, *Exodus!*, 162.

57. Lackey, "Moses, Man of Oppression," 582–83.

58. Gooding-Williams, "Politics, Racial Solidarity, Exodus!," 124.

59. Gooding-Williams, 124. Robert J. Patterson also offers an insightful contribution to the debate. He claims that Black male proponents of the discourse

"collapse the categories" of gender, sexuality, race, and class "in ways that inhibit communal empowerment." See Patterson, *Exodus Politics*, 7.

60. Marbury, *Pillars of Cloud and Fire*, 189.

61. Marbury, 189.

62. Marbury, 200.

63. See Walzer and Said, "An Exchange"; and Said, "Michael Walzer's 'Exodus.'"

64. Walzer and Said, 253.

65. Walzer and Said, 253.

66. Walzer and Said, 255. Delores Williams, author of *Sisters in the Wilderness*, criticizes Black theology of liberation for the same reason Said criticizes Walzer: without a serious investigation into why God frees one group at the expense of another group's freedom, liberation theologians are hard pressed to claim their God as liberatory.

67. Diner, *Julius Rosenwald*.

68. Goldstein, *Price of Whiteness*, 72.

69. Du Bois, "As the crow flies, December 7, 1940."

70. Anderson, *Bourgeois Radicals*, 7.

71. The Bronx Slave Market was first documented by Baker and Cooke, "Bronx Slave Market," in Adams and Bracey, *Strangers and Neighbors*.

72. James, "Ella Baker," 12.

73. James, 12.

74. Smith, "Rock and a Hard Place," 7–9.

75. Goldstein, Price of Whiteness, 36.

76. Berman, "American Jews," 411.

77. Goldstein, *Price of Whiteness*, 195.

78. Dollinger, *Black Power, Jewish Politics*, 3.

79. Cheryl Greenberg, "Black-Jewish Relations and the Rise and Fall of Liberalism," *USA Today*, May 1, 2000, 33.

80. Cruse, *Crisis of the Negro Intellectual*, 480.

81. Cruse, 483.

82. Chazan, "Fallacies of Pragmatism," in Washington, *Jews in Black Perspectives*, 148.

83. Chazan, 151. The relationship between Israel and South Africa was reignited in 1974 following three crucial events: the Yom Kippur War of 1973, which was the fourth war between Israel and Arab-led forces, and an unsuccessful attempt to win back the Golan Heights; the Arab oil embargo, which cooled relations between Israel and the United States and Europe; and, with the exception of four African nations, the continent of Africa's cutting of diplomatic

ties to Israel. All of this led to the restoration of diplomatic relations between South Africa and Israel (151–52). The relationship chiefly involved the economy (South Africa exported 50 percent of its steel to Israel, and Israel invested in the apartheid nation's diamonds and financial investments) and politics (South Africa provided weapons to Israel and proved to be potentially a more reliable ally than the United States, which criticized Israel). Chazan, 160–63.

84. Chazan, 149.

85. Feldman, *Shadow over Palestine*, 187.

86. Dollinger, *Quest for Inclusion*, 20. Dollinger also argues that the New Deal created the conditions for the "American Jewish dream"—namely, "integration into the mainstream"—to surface.

87. The New Deal was not as financially beneficial to African Americans, writes Paul Moreno in "Ambivalent Legacy."

88. Dollinger, *Quest for Inclusion*, 18. We must keep in mind that the federal assistance that fueled Jewish financial and political success exceeded by far the benefits received by African Americans.

89. Lewis, "Shortcuts to the Mainstream," in Washington, *Jews in Black Perspectives*, 96.

90. However, we must not forget the federal barriers that prevented Blacks from acquiring access to home mortgages and business loans between the end of the Cold War and the early 1970s.

91. Jacobson's *Barbarian Virtues* offers a formidable argument regarding the rise of the American Empire. He writes that this empire stemmed from and was built on immigration and the cheap labor it provided to the nation; likewise, "foreign" territories were needed to consume the nation's products, setting the backdrop to the emergence of the United States as a world empire. The United States's justification for entering foreign territories stemmed from Theodore Roosevelt's foreign policy, which depicted the United States as benevolent and omniscient in liberating countries from their barbaric and uncivilized past and showing them the way to a civilized future.

92. Gil Steinlauf, "Jews in America Struggled for Decades to Become White. Now We Must Give up Whiteness to Fight Racism," *Washington Post*, September 22, 2015.

93. Please see Walzer's *Exodus and Revolution*. He writes, "Exodus is a big story, one that became part of the cultural consciousness of the West—so that a range of political events . . . have been located and understood within the narrative frame that it provides" (7).

94. Heschel, "Religion and Race."

4

Teaching Blacks and Jews in 2020

TJ: Jacques, we've been teaching the Blacks and Jews in America course for five years running. What has surprised you the most about the class?

JB: One of the most surprising things we've learned while teaching our Blacks and Jews in America course is that our students have no idea that our syllabus is about the *relation* between Blacks and Jews in America. Many thought it would consist of two separate components: a "Blacks" module and a "Jews" module. You know, that it would be like a general education (gen ed) requirement, a diversity requirement, or so on. They had no idea an actual *relationship* between these two peoples existed and stretched back throughout American history.

What do you make of their lack of awareness of the lengthy and complex historical encounter between these two minority groups?

TJ: Our Black and Jewish students seem to be invisible to each other. Many of them grew up in deeply segregated and homogeneous communities, places shaped along narrowly construed lines of race and class. It's highly unlikely that a significant portion of our Jewish and Black students would have encountered each other in social or academic settings—that is, in the same advanced placement class, attending the same pool party, sharing notes in a study group. This social disconnect is irreparable.

JB: I sometimes fear you're right. This disconnect might be irreparable—as in, they will still be strangers to one another forty years from now.

TJ: Blacks and Jews at this historical moment would appear to be as far apart as immigrant Jews were from elite white gentiles when the former came to the United States in the nineteenth century. Existing social, religious, and economic structures make it nearly impossible for young people from these groups to connect or even to *see* each other as anything other than strangers.

Secondary schools aren't teaching the complex history of race and rights in the United States or any other narrative that would highlight the historic encounters between Blacks and white Jews. How, then, do we expect these students to discover any connections between them at a meta or micro level?

JB: True. Then again, there are no two groups in this country that have had so much solidarity and so much strife between them. They have had so much interaction. My point is that if secondary schools were to teach an interethnic module, "Blacks and Jews in America" would have a ready-made syllabus. It would cover everything from James Baldwin to bell hooks, Norman Podhoretz to Letty Pogrebin. Do you agree?

TJ: Of course. But your expectations are unusually high for an institution already suffocating from unaddressed economic disparities and the so-called achievement gap among students of different racial and economic backgrounds. Your argument also places a great deal of faith in our collective ability to do the heavy lifting that is required to teach a course on Blacks and Jews in America. As you well know, the historic interethnic encounters in the United States exposes a disturbing narrative of Christianity's role in perpetuating anti-Black racism and antisemitism. Do you really believe high school history teachers would garner the administrative support needed to teach such a class?

Notwithstanding the instructional gap's impact on the rich history of interethnic studies, white Jewish flight to the middle-class suburbs underscores the critical point I have been struggling to articulate: Blacks and Jews are invisible to each other by choice. Please convince me otherwise.

JB: I agree. They are invisible by choice. And they became invisible by cultural structures that made their choices not to engage with one another seem "natural," in the sense that Antonio Gramsci used the word.

It wasn't always that way. In the aftermath of the Great Migration, Blacks and Jews lived near one another in northern urban enclaves. They certainly knew one another, though they didn't necessarily get along that well. Ditto in the 1930s and 1940s when they met one another in communist movements. Probably around the 1950s is when they started physically moving away from one another. The paradox is that this—and by "this," I am referring to Jewish white flight to the suburbs—coincides with the so-called Golden Era, when elites in both groups worked on numerous civil rights issues together. At the very moment they were winning these victories for racial justice, they were actually in the process of physically distancing themselves.

So our students are indeed surprised to learn the relationship wasn't always the way it is now. They didn't know that there was a backstory. They didn't even know there was a *story*.

Nowadays, Terrence, where do our Black students organically come across Jews and vice versa?

TJ: Unfortunately, there's no organic encounter between them in any intimate setting. Their relationship is primarily transactional. In a general sense, many of our working-class African American students may live in homes or apartments owned by Jewish landlords. Maybe one of their coaches or teachers is Jewish. African American middle-class students may have overheard a parent's discussion regarding a Jewish boss or the number of Jews in positions of power at his or her workplace.

Something similar can be said of our Jewish students. If the only Black woman they know, for instance, is their nanny, it is safe to assume that experience will inform their subsequent relations with other Black women.

Please keep in mind, just as urban myths are consumed at white suburban dinner tables about allegedly "unqualified" African Americans getting into Harvard, about the Black "welfare queen," and about Black men dating white women, there exists in many Black communities parallel anecdotes of white Jews as being über successful, both academically and financially. If the students' initial point of engaging each other is through stereotypical anecdotes, we should expect a contentious classroom until we, as so-called educators, make every effort to address such preexisting beliefs about each other. Obviously, what I am saying is not new to you.

JB: Ha! No, it's not new. But it's not contentious at Georgetown University, where everyone is so gosh darn friendly and doing the head nod I alluded to earlier. Eventually you and I do get under the students' skin, as it were, and they start to open up.

I think the lack of Jewish exposure to Black compatriots is a function of class, and that, of course, intersects with race. As the Jewish community grew more affluent, Jewish children were increasingly likely to attend expensive private schools. (I am not speaking here of Orthodox Jews, who attend their own schools, which are not expensive but are exclusively for Orthodox Jews.) These institutions all predictably fail to look anything like the nation at large. As for Jews in *public* schools, their attendance is also a dynamic inflected by class. The public schools they attend are usually in the wealthiest districts, where the percentage of African American students is well below the 14 percent mark of the national population.

Where else might Black and Jewish kids come across each other in the contemporary United States?

TJ: Black kids and white Jewish kids don't often cross paths in the real world. Yes, they may rub shoulders in the locker room or on the soccer field, but that's it. Jewish kids are more likely to peer into

Black life through rap music and popular culture than to engage a Black kid over lunch or dinner.

The same can't be said of African Americans. I can't think of any corresponding medium through which Black kids might peer into the lives of white Jewish kids.

The intimacy you wish to see among Blacks and Jews only exists within literature. For instance, James McBride's *The Color of Water* provides a curious but stark understanding of Black-Jewish encounters.[1] The price of such intimacy is a form of death. In McBride's autobiography, his mom is estranged from her Jewish family after she marries a Black man. She is dead to her family, especially to her dad. Her Jewish identity is dead. And she symbolically wraps herself in a new identity as a Black Christian woman. As far as the reader can tell, no one questions her racial identity. Her neighbors and the parents of her children's classmates assume she is Black because of her children's phenotype. It's a disturbing but classic story in many working-class Black communities: The annihilation of one's ethnic identity is the norm rather than the exception.

This is why, if you want to get the real scoop of our families, you need to attend an African American funeral. Unknown children and partners will always surface, and a few of them will be white and Jewish.

JB: In our class, we often have a substantial proportion of students who are neither Black nor Jewish. They seem oddly fascinated by it all. Many Asian American students, in particular, tell us that the whole experience is mind-blowing. They tell me that when they hear about the assimilation of the Jews in the United States, they are reminded of a role they have now been forced to play—that of the model minority. They feel pitted against Black and Brown people in subtle and not-so-subtle ways.

TJ: I think there's another reason why some Asian Americans take our class. I don't believe all immigrants are forced into the category of "model minority." Immigrants pursue and reinvent the category to different purposes. When Caribbean and African immigrants come to the United States, for instance, their parents often forbid them to associate with African Americans as they are perceived as being at the bottom of the academic ladder. The parents' goal is to have their child(ren) emulate the best students in the classroom—specifically, they identify the Asian immigrants and the Jews.

As far as I can tell, Asian Americans have also sought out model minorities—namely, the Jews. In an effort to widen their political reach, according to a 2007 *New York Times* article, Asian American leaders have also turned to Jews for assistance.[2] Our course feeds into these students' curiosity as to how Jews have succeeded as a religious minority.

> **JB:** Have you noticed that in our Blacks and Jews class, whenever we get to the unit on Afro-Jews, something seems to change? It's as if all of the tensions dissipate. I think the vibe changes for both groups.
>
> What do you think is going on in the hearts and minds of our non-Jewish African American students?

TJ: I can't give you an answer. It's as if our Black students are closeted Afrocentric activists until we reach our section on Afro-Jews, at which point they bask in their true identity. Let's face it, whenever Africa or *Blackness* is acknowledged and legitimated within ancient civilization and in one of the world's most important monotheistic traditions, most Black students will find a reason to celebrate. How often is Blackness or Africa noted for epistemic inventions?

In a more serious tone, introducing Judaism's rich diversity is yet another reminder of our imaginative limits in the United States, where a stark white-Black racial binary strangles our imaginative possibilities. Of course, Jews are "racially" and phenotypically diverse people, and not through conversion; but in the United States, Jews and Judaism are portrayed as European and phenotypically white, even though we all know Israel sits on the shoulders of Africa. Lewis Gordon really nails it in his article "Rarely Kosher: Studying Jews of Color in North America," where he gives us a historical understanding of the emergence of a democratically diverse group of people who identify with the tribe.[3]

White Jewish students, however, don't seem to be surprised or bothered by the readings, and that troubles me. Within the context of the course, which dives into the weeds of structural racism and insidious attacks against Jews by white elites, I expected a different response from the students. I wanted them to express outrage, excitement, confusion—something. Otherwise, what's the point of pursuing knowledge and discovering new aspects of one's ancestry and tradition?

JB: I think the Jewish kids *are* initially shocked. At first, they seem bemused by black Judaism and Black Judaism (see chapter 2). Then they experience a sense of relief because throughout the semester they are hammered for the thoughtless manner in which they benefit from their white skin privilege. All of a sudden, they realize their religion is incredibly diverse. When you and I start assigning work about various forms of Afro-Judaism, I do think a lot of the Jewish kids undergo a good old-fashioned paradigm shift.

One proviso: Sephardic Jews (who only infrequently attend Georgetown) are not shocked at all. We Sephardic Jews (I'm half Sephardic) grew up with people of color in our families, so Afro-Jews aren't in any way unusual.

TJ: For African Americans, it's not a redemption but a form of recovery when they encounter Afro-Jews. Their existence in a world that refuses to see and acknowledge them is an extension of anti-Black racism operating at a global level. When Black students meet Afro-Jews in scholarly writings, they discover something about themselves as well. No longer is anti-Blackness a figment of their imagination or a symbol of victimization; instead, Afro-Jews signify the rich fluidity of identity. They present a picture of what is undeniably human—our depth, reach, and possibility—and the students can see themselves beyond the boundaries of white supremacy.

JB: So when our class is done, and we read through ours students' fifty or sixty final papers, what do you think has changed for them from day one when they walked in, thinking it was some sort of modular gen ed course?

TJ: I think it varies and depends on the students' political and so-cial orientation. I think for half the class, the students leave over-whelmed and with information that they can't really process in any meaningful way. Unfortunately, the academy, with its increasing professionalization, does not provide an outlet for grappling with this religious and racial problem.

For the remaining half, I think they choose to ignore the truthful-ness of white privilege.

What do you think changes?

JB: I have had the most intense post-class discussions with white Jew-ish students. Nine out of every ten have said the entire experience was staggering—as in it shifted some of their basic thinking about Judaism. For instance, they are usually Ashkenazi and thus have the haziest understanding of even Sephardic Jews, let alone Black Juda-ism. To them, Judaism is white, yet they seem relieved to know that it's not just white.

Then I find a handful of non-Jewish Black students doing the pre-professional thing—which is precisely what they should be doing—and asking me to write letters of recommendation for law school or to network them with people I know in fields that interest them. I find that very satisfying. I'd like to think the contents of the class made them see me as an ally and a mentor in their professional endeavors.

TJ: Sometimes I wonder if I'm failing the Black students who take our class. A handful of Jewish students will routinely return to my office hours long after the class has ended. Most of them are search-ing for ways to connect the readings to their own social activism and scholarly aspirations after college.

I can't recall the last time a Black student from the class con-tacted me to discuss Black-Jewish relations. When they return to my office hours, it's to rehearse federal policies designed to keep Blacks economically disenfranchised or to tell me how the readings intro-duced them to a world of structural racisms that they didn't know existed prior to the class.

I am not interested in reproducing Black-Jewish partnerships that mirror the 1960s, but on some level, I want the material to initiate some degree of political or cultural intimacy between strangers who embrace a similar Exodus story in America.

Are you satisfied with our class as we've executed it to date? I think we need to expand the geographic boundaries of our scholarly readings to include encounters between Blacks and Jews in places such as Brazil, France, and South Africa. Are you amenable to this?

JB: First, on the partnerships between students, I, too, wish there were Black-Jewish partnerships among the students taking the class. But we go back to our original point: Choices are the residue of social structure, and the social structures do not make it easy for these kids to form partnerships. I guess some of the African American and Jewish American students date, though I am reminded of Patricia Williams's important piece in which she wondered why Americans are so eager to resolve social conflicts through sex and romance.[4] But, like you, I don't have a clear sense of the students' building partnerships after the semester is over.

As for extending our reach to include Brazil, France, and South Africa, I like that idea, though we would both need to get in the field and talk to people. The university likely wouldn't support us to spend a year in Paris or Johannesburg. I'm not sure our families would warm to the idea either!

But, yes, you're right. The next step in *Blacks and Jews studies should focus on their relations outside of the United States.

Notes

1. McBride, *Color of Water.*

2. Neela Banerjee, "In Jews, Indian-Americans See a Role Model in Activism," *New York Times*, October 2, 2007, https://www.nytimes.com/2007/10/02/us/02hindu.html?searchResultPosition=9.

3. Gordon, "Rarely Kosher."

4. Williams, "On Imagining Foes," in Salzman and West, *Struggles in the Promised Land.*

5

Interview with Professor Susannah Heschel

JB: Professor Heschel, the image of your father marching arm in arm with Ralph Bunche and Dr. Martin Luther King Jr. during the 1965 March in Selma, Alabama, may be just the most iconic visual image in modern American Judaism. I sometimes wonder if all those Jewish kids in their Hebrew schools who see that photo on their classroom whiteboard understand the significance of that image. I wonder if they understand what your father did and what your father risked.

SH: I agree that the photograph from Selma is iconic. Yet while many Jews view that photograph as a mark of pride in their Jewishness, I always tell them, "No, this is a photograph that should be a challenge to you!" As long as racism remains so pervasive in our society, including in the Jewish community, I'm not certain if the Jewish community deserves to have that photograph, at least not until there is commitment to massive change.

JB: The march itself was about voting rights, correct?

SH: Right. In a way, it was a celebration. It was not Bloody Sunday but a couple of weeks later, with federal troops now protecting the marchers and with people from around the United States and even other countries joining the march. It was about voting rights and the Voting Rights Act that was passed by Congress. Still, it was very dangerous to go to Alabama and march for civil rights, and I was afraid when my father left home for Selma, worried that I might never see him again. At the time, I didn't hear people in the Jewish community praising his involvement in civil rights. On the contrary, I remember quite distinctly that it took until around 1979 or 1980 before I finally began to hear Jews saying, "I'm so glad your father went to Selma."

So let's fast forward to the present moment. What kind of courage does it take today to speak out against what some state legislatures and the Supreme Court have done to eviscerate the Voting Rights Act? No one is asking people to march across the [Edmund] Pettus Bridge. No one is asking them to face Sheriff Jim Clark, or "Bull" Connor—just to raise a voice. Where is the American Jewish community on this?

TJ: What I am hearing from you is a challenge to the Jewish community. Some Jews would argue that they have risen to the challenge. That they have remained allies. That they have raised their voices.

SH: You know, it's such a complex problem. In the famous photograph of the Selma march, way in the background, just as they're beginning to walk on the bridge, you can see a sign that says "Teppers." That was a department store in Selma owned by a Jew who was very opposed to the civil rights movement. He was an arch segregationist.

JB: Oh God, Sol Tepper. Rabbis who knew him tell me stories about him. I think he was on the White Citizens Council!

SH: Correct. So having that name in the background of the photo—it's on my computer—is a reminder to me. True, there were a lot of Jewish organizations that honored Dr. King, but there were a lot of Jewish organizations that submitted amicus briefs in support of [1978 *Regents of the University of California v.*] *Bakke* in opposition to affirmative action.

A few years later, Jesse Jackson said something that was inappropriate. He referred to New York City as "Hymie Town." It's not appropriate. Then again, it's not the worst thing I've heard. I've studied antisemitism. I would say on a scale of one to a thousand, it's more like a one or a two, when a thousand is the worst. And Jesse Jackson apologized.

One of my friends, Joan Martin, an African American theologian, said to me, "Why don't the Jews accept his apology?" I have no answer for that.

So when you want to talk about allies, the first thing with an ally is you accept an apology. That's called friendship.

JB: On this idea of Jews turning their backs on folks who share a lot in common with them, do you notice in contemporary Judaism a strange form of moral equivalence where the actions of a white supremacist who murders Jews in a synagogue are paralleled to somewhat objectionable statements made by, let's say, a member of "The Squad"? You know what incident I'm referring to? And the reaction is, "Oh, look at what Representative Ilhan Omar said." "A scandal like this has never occurred in all of Israel!" Et cetera.

Do Jews need to be more discerning?

SH: Absolutely. So in October 2018, just days before the shooting at the Tree of Life Synagogue, the *American Historical Review* published a group of articles about antisemitism. And one of them was by Professor Scott Ury from Israel. He talked about the politicization of the study of antisemitism—what "counts" as antisemitic and how left- and right-wing positions affect our scholarship, manipulating antisemitism for political purposes. So, yes, antisemitism has become highly politicized, which is outrageous.

After the Tree of Life Synagogue shooting by a racist white nationalist, Jews were devastated. How could such an attack against Jews in a synagogue happen in America?

I wanted to say to them, "You don't know what America is."

TJ: What didn't they know about America?

SH: They don't understand that there is also an America where arsonists burn Black churches to the ground, where white racists march into a church's Bible study and kill people, where white people go to church and then torture and lynch Black men, women, and children. This has a long history. But because Jews identify with white people, they fail to recognize this America.

JB: Well, since we're talking about events that happened in the South, Professor Johnson and I switched to different textbooks this year, and the new one concentrated a lot on southern Judaism. Teaching it, as opposed to just reading it, was a different experience. So, on the one hand, we have your father, in the prophetic tradition, with Reverend Martin Luther King Jr. But there's a counter story in the Blacks and Jews narrative. It's a story about the not-always-good behavior of Jews in the South.

SH: To quote the title of Michael Rothberg's new book, *The Implicated Subject*, we're all implicated.[1] I also love Karen Brodkin's book *How Jews Became White Folks*.[2] She makes very important points about the advantages Jews have had as whites to move into the suburbs after World War II and about the racism that kept African Americans out of the suburbs. But the Jews didn't just become white in the twentieth century. They became white when German Jews arrived here in the nineteenth century and ignored the existence of slavery while proclaiming America the land of freedom. East European, Yiddish-speaking Jews arrived much later and were horrified by lynchings, which they called pogroms.

Some Jews were attentive to racism, others not. And this is not new. Think about the Jewish philosopher [Baruch] Spinoza. He lived in seventeenth-century Amsterdam, a slave-trading port city, and his family was involved in international trade and without question knew about the slave trade. Yet no one who writes about Spinoza ever asks why he didn't speak against slavery. He was surrounded by it. He saw it. He wrote about ethics. He wrote philosophy!

But more troubling is that of all the many scholars who write books about Spinoza, only one author that I know of, Willi Goetschel, has talked about Spinoza and the Amsterdam slave trade.[3] Why do the scholars not address this, given that every few months there's a new book or article about Spinoza? Are we as oblivious as he was?

TJ: I'm wondering, are you holding the Jewish community to a particular standard that speaks to what you elsewhere called "a theo-political vision of the prophets"? From reading scholars such as Eric Goldstein, I've come to consider the complicated history of white Jews as perennially the other but not necessarily marginalized within American society.[4] Jews may have been welcomed, as somewhat white, but they also knew that at any moment they could be shipped off as well.

So I'm just wondering, are you holding Jews accountable to a high standard, expecting them to be a "chosen people" in their dealings with Blacks?

SH: What can I say? The Jewish philosopher Maimonides, who was no liberal, said that slavery is immoral. How then did the Bible permit it? Maimonides argued that in biblical times, people were at a lower moral level, and God needed to accommodate us. Yet if Maimonides could recognize in the twelfth century that slavery was immoral, it's very hard for me to accept that Spinoza in the seventeenth century or the Jews in America in the nineteenth century could not.

TJ: I want to go back to this idea of the prophets and the prophetic tradition. Your father and Dr. King were very aware of those traditions. You've written that even though SNCC took a leftist turn away from the SCLC [Southern Christian Leadership Conference] and turned to what SNCC called Third World politics, its members still found ways to incorporate Negro spirituals and images of the Hebrew Bible within their public speeches and political platforms.

I'm wondering, as you not only listen to the words of Black Lives Matter activists but also take in the images that we're seeing among this generation of civil rights activists, is the Old Testament tradition of prophecy still operative? What are the potential shortfalls or up-sides of not having that imagery within our political imagination right now?

SH: My father completed his doctoral dissertation on the prophets at the University of Berlin in December 1932. Hitler came to power the next month. Some antisemitic Protestant theologians in Germany wanted the Old Testament removed from the Christian Bible.

My father came to the United States in 1940 to teach. Imagine what it meant to him that Dr. King made the prophetic tradition the center of the civil rights movement. Notice that in Dr. King's major public speeches, he rarely spoke about Jesus and the Sermon on the Mount but quoted the Hebrew prophets.

The motto at the Civil Rights Memorial in Montgomery, Alabama, is a verse from Amos. That is extraordinary!

TJ: It is extraordinary. Indeed, enslaved Africans, as you know, found resources from biblical prophets to create a radical biblical hermeneutics. Some could make the case that the Hebrew Bible played a far more consequential role in the civil rights movement than the New Testament.

SH: And I think the reason is this: The prophets understand despair. Unless you understand the depths of despair, your hope sounds superficial, ludicrous. It's irrelevant. I don't want to hear hope from someone who doesn't understand my despair. So I think for someone who is in despair, the first thing he or she needs is to be understood in all dimensions of suffering, in the depths.

We have that in the Hasidic tradition, and it's something my father drew from also. It's prophetic, and it's Hasidic. In Hasidic tradition, a main issue is, how should a rebbe respond to someone in despair? What is the nature of despair? Why do people fall into despair, and how do you lift them out?

The first thing is, you have to feel their own despair with them; the rebbe must descend into the other person's despair, feel it, experience it. You can't argue with someone in despair and say, "Oh, well, cheer up, things are not so bad, could be worse," or such platitudes.

I think the prophets understand, because they speak with such a passionate voice, screaming about suffering and injustice. And then they are able to give us a messianic hope, a hope for redemption.

TJ: Do you find that despair is absent from our public conversations on police brutality? When I replay in my head Eric Garner's cry, "I can't breathe," I hear despair. When I remember Sandra Bland's arrest on the Texas highway, listening to the tone of her voice in the video replay, I hear despair.

I'm wondering, has that despair now beckoned us, on the one hand, to finally embrace Black Lives Matter? And on the other hand, does it render us silent as we try to incorporate despair into a transformative social vision?

SH: I think it is a challenge to each of us to hear, "I can't breathe." It's a demand, asking us, "Are you a human being? Are you a human being? Because I can't breathe. Are you going to do something? Are you going to help me? Or are you not a human being? Are you dead?"

And we are in so many ways dead. Not responding? That's a dead person.

TJ: We are increasingly growing numb to these images. As I prepared for this interview, I listened to a 1972 NBC interview with your father and returned to King's "Letter from Birmingham Jail." What's striking is the robust conception of what it means to be human. Despite characterizing racism and antisemitism, according to your dad, as diseases within our society, both men didn't flinch when they proclaimed they could see the humanity, if only a glimmer of it, within the persons who committed evil acts against Blacks and Jews. Not that I'm going to embrace their claim wholeheartedly, but nonetheless I will recognize profound truthfulness in it.

Have we lost that capacity to see the humanity in others, especially within the evil perpetrators of violence against our people?

Without Heschel's and King's vision, or a corresponding vision, we don't seem to possess the vocabulary needed to create a political imagination beyond death and despair.

SH: I agree. I agree. You asked me about Black Lives Matter in the absence of the prophetic tradition. You used the word "numb." I know what you mean, and I agree with you, but I also just think people are dead.

There were people standing there, whether it was Eric Garner or George Floyd or Sandra Bland. People who stood there.

You know, there is no such thing as a bystander. No one "stands by." "Bystander" is a word that has no action to it. To stand and watch, to do nothing, to say nothing—you are dying. You are dead if you're just standing there. You're making yourself a dead person.

So, yes, I think that the Black Lives Matter movement, to me, is a kind of resurrection moment, with people affirming life and saying "No! Come alive, people!" Think of what happened to Michael Brown in Ferguson.

So is there a religious element to Black Lives Matter? I'm not sure I have an answer right now for that. I would like to see it. I would like to say that to stand up and demonstrate, to speak out like that is, in fact, a religious moment in the prophetic tradition, whether or not the words of the prophets are quoted. It feels to me very much like a resurrection moment, saying, "No, you tried to kill all of us when you did this! You tried to destroy us, destroy our souls, our hearts, our conscience! A mass murder! And we are not going to allow that to happen."

TJ: The last question takes us back to the 2018 massacre at the Tree of Life Synagogue in Pittsburgh. I was shocked to discover in article after article the number of columnists and Jewish leaders who identified Minister Louis Farrakhan, the spiritual leader of the Nation of Islam, as a major factor in the spread of antisemitism in the United States and subsequently a contributing factor to white supremist attacks against American Jews. With fewer than fifty thousand official members in the Nation of Islam—the size of two

Black megachurches in Dallas—why do you think Minister Farra-khan plays an outsize role in the imaginations of many American Jews? His name is referenced whenever a Black athlete or entertainer spews a blunder or off-the-cuff reference to Jewish financial success or conspiracy theory of Jewish power and influence within the media, sports, and entertainment industries.

Interestingly enough, many of my white Jewish students tell me they have never listened to any of his speeches, but in their minds, he's the face of American antisemitism.

I'm curious. Why does Minister Farrakhan continue to loom large in countless Jewish communities during a moment when BLM activists hardly ever mention him or any other religious figure, for that matter?

SH: I think what Farrakhan said was demagoguery.[5] He's a dema-gogue. And there are outrageous things that have been said by other demagogues. One of them got elected president, which is pretty shocking. But what Farrakhan said was so outrageous and so much echoing Nazi language at a time when Jews were building a Holo-caust museum and memorials around the country and interviewing the last living survivors and so on. For him to say that was really, really nasty and terribly hurtful. And I don't want to give an analogy, but I can imagine what it is like to be raped and have the policemen say, "Well, look how you were dressed," or something like that. That really goes to the core of a person's soul.

Why would Farrakhan choose to say such things about Jews and Judaism? And why would anybody resonate to it? Why wouldn't people just pick up and say, "Goodbye, I'm outta here"?

So the problem is not just that he said it, but that people didn't walk away and that he got attention for his antisemitism. He knew he could get attention and be in the newspapers for saying some-thing naughty, outrageous. People like scandals, and newspapers report about it. So he picked on something that was especially hurt-ful, and he did it in a way to get attention to himself, and he persisted with it. He won't stop, and not enough people are walking away from him.

JB: So how should Jews respond to him?

SH: I don't think anybody knows how to respond to demagoguery. We don't know how to respond to Trump. We're all, whether it's the Lincoln Project or Anderson Cooper, struggling with what to do. Do you mock? Do you yell? Do you scold? What do we do? Do you ignore it?

Jews don't want to ignore Farrakhan any more than African Americans want to ignore a racist. But the other problem is that Farrakhan is not Mr. Black America. He's not the voice of African Americans. So making it as such, that's on the other side; that's a problem. Why do Jews credit him in that way?

We have so many allies and friends in the African American community. Let's focus on them and on being good allies and friends ourselves. We have a great heritage that we should always remember.

Notes

1. Rothberg, *Implicated Subject.*
2. Brodkin, *How Jews Became White Folks.*
3. Goetschel, "Spinoza's Dream."
4. Goldstein, *Price of Whiteness.*
5. For additional information on Farrakhan's public references to Jews, please see Berman's introduction in Berman, *Blacks and Jews*, 1–28.

6

Interview with Professor Yvonne Chireau

TJ: Professor Chireau, I'm always curious as to the motivation behind a scholar's work and why he or she pursues a particular scholarly or vocational path. What inspired you to assemble the noteworthy volume you edited (with Nathaniel Deutsch) titled *Black Zion: African American Religious Encounters with Judaism*?[1] It's a great scholarly resource and a major contribution to the academic study of African American religions.

YC: Thank you. Yes, this is a good question. As a young religionist with a specialty in African American religions, I was really concerned about some of the gaps in the scholarship. So when I wrote my first book, *Black Magic: Religion and the African American Conjuring Tradition*, I was like, "Oh, no one is talking about folk magic as a strand of African American religions."[2] A similar thing happened with this notion of Black religions and Judaism. I viewed it as another facet of African American religious experiences.

The question for me at the time was, Why do we privilege Christianity, and specifically Protestant Christianity, in the study of African American religions? Yes, it makes sense in light of the pivotal role of the Black church, but I never found that to be a good starting point from which to study religions. I'm interested in Black religion, wherever and however it lands. So that was my first motive: I wanted to highlight spiritual diversity and religious pluralism in African American life.

TJ: As you were editing *Black Zion*, do you recall a revelatory moment or astounding argument that opened your eyes to an otherwise-overlooked aspect of religion in general and African American religions in particular?

YC: My coeditor and I knew that we didn't want the book to be about "Black and Jewish relations." So we framed it in terms of religious encounter, which is something that we understood as what happens when religious ideas and expressions come together in a kind of dynamic process. We put out the call for the collection, and I was concerned about what kinds of submissions we would receive. But the revelation was that other people understood exactly what we were trying to do. They understood that in real terms there isn't such a thing as "correct" practices or ideas in the study of religion.

We found, with Black Jews and Black Hebrews and Black Israelites, this idea in the scholarship that they weren't "really" Jews. Still to this day, we hear this: "Oh, they're not authentic Jews." There was a notion that there's some sort of normative religion, and everything apart from that is heterodox, abnormal, strange.

I've never upheld that notion. It doesn't work well in the study of religion.

And I remember one reviewer said, "Well, basically these are cults, and they're idiosyncratic." I thought that this was the wrong attitude. The concept of the cult has been used to marginalize some of the most interesting religious movements because they are seen as deviating from the norms. In the book we wanted to legitimate, at least in our scholarship, the reality of African American encounters with both Jews and variations of Judaism that have been historically present.

TJ: The volume was published in 2000. In my estimation, it was and remains a visionary collection of essays that underscored the depth and substance of an important narrative within American religion—that of Afro-Jews. Of well-known African American Jews, a few names from the entertainment field immediately come to mind: Tiffany Haddish, Drake, Alicia Garza, Daveed Diggs, Maya Rudolph, and Lenny Kravitz. Many more African Americans are discussing their Jewish roots in ways I don't recall happening with the previous generation of entertainers, which included Sammy Davis Jr. and Nell Carter.

As your research shows, Afro-Jews have been with us for generations. What has fueled the popular discussions of Afro-Jews between 2000 and 2020? What do you think is the single biggest change in the way the public recognizes Jews of African American ancestry?

YC: The biggest thing is that Afro-Jews are not anomalous. You know, back in the day, you'd try to think of a Black Jewish person, and all you'd come up with is Sammy Davis Jr. Today there are Black Jews as public figures, and they're not considered outsiders or cult members. There's more acceptance.

One of the differences is that today I don't think it matters as much. It's not striking and strange. "Oh, this is just another part of one's identity, one's brand." And to my view, it doesn't matter that much. Whereas there was a period before when people such as Sammy Davis Jr. or Julius Lester were seen as unusual exceptions as Black religious persons, "Black Jews" as a category has expanded today to include Black Hebrews, those practicing Black Israelite religions, and so forth. But to be sure, these groups have been with us [in the United States] since the nineteenth century.

Today, there are more Black Jews who are claiming political space, and that's somewhat different than it was back then. Some of these people, who might be either Jews from birth or converts to Judaism, might be seen as we see Black Protestants—just practicing another version of Christianity, nothing out of the ordinary. For others, particularly those who are seen as insurgent or problematic in terms of racial identity, the question remains, How do we understand these groups and their religious experiences, and how do they understand themselves?

TJ: Could you say more? As you may know, actor and talk show host Nick Cannon faced fierce public criticism and was called an antisemite during the summer of 2020 after he proclaimed on his radio show that Blacks were the true Semitic people. His argument dates back to the nineteenth-century debate among Black scholars on Africa's presence in antiquity and biblical times.

Who are the *real* Semites?

YC: The Nick Cannons of the world are clear: "No, I'm Black, but I am a Semite." What does that mean? And what does that do for Black people politically, for someone like Nick Cannon?

This is why we need to study Black religion as religion and take it more seriously: These conversations have been engaged by African Americans since the early nineteenth century, even during slavery. We have Black intellectuals who were trying to make sense of this important question of who are the real Jews, the original Semites, the Israelites of the Bible. These questions have been raised for so long as African American political and religious discourses cohered to give meaning to Black identity. And yet, these voices have been overlooked, ignored, forgotten. And then, when the issues is raised again later, people think it's a new issue.

So I think the first thing we have to do is recover these genealogies and race histories as religious narratives that show how Black folk have been theorizing and speculating on these themes all along. These narratives of identity are religious stories that transmit sacred histories and accounts of the Black Israelite religions, lost tribes, African Jews, Ethiopianism, and so forth.

TJ: What are they drawing on?

YC: So when Nick Cannon or these modern interpreters of Blackness and Semitic origins speak like this, they're drawing upon a legacy of interpretation that's really extensive in African American culture. They're drawing upon the work of preachers, theologians, artists, and so forth who have done their own research.

Now I hear the critics saying, "Well, what kind of research is that? Is it professional? Is it historical?" Well, some of it is, and some of it isn't, but what they're doing is making a claim to the inspiring myths of the racial and spiritual origins of a people. That kind of work has been going on and on for centuries in the sermons and speeches and writings of African American religious thinkers. And it's been sort of under the radar. But now it's even more public, which I'm delighted about because I think there's a lot of confusion about these histories as being something that Black folk just made up. No, these works are rooted in the formation of memory and history that ties closely with the creation of racial mythologies. They're not just suddenly invented by people who scream it on the corner. They are deeply held and cherished sacred stories that have been transmitted for generations.

So again, I think there's this sort of devaluation and diminishing of theorizing and speculation by African Americans on their own histories. We know that from the earliest, Black folk have been adept at creating religious forms that draw upon a fount of expressive genius, as W. E. B. DuBois told us.

This is where I hear the critics saying, "Well, that's not history, that's not history." Well, what do you think religion is? Religion is about creating and enacting myths to live with, and inhabiting the stories that are most meaningful.

I think it's a good thing that these ideas are becoming more public. But they have always been with us.

JB: So in your volume *Black Zion*, there is a piece by Bernard Wolfson that is really interesting.[3] It lingers on Rabbi Capers Funnye, a black Jew *and* a Black Jew and a person I really want to meet some day. Rabbi Funnye has been making a very kind offer throughout his entire career, and he made it in the Wolfson piece as well: He wants to serve as a bridge in the Blacks and Jews dialogue. I think he's absolutely right, except nobody's using him as a bridge, right? I mean here and there, yes, but he has so much more to offer. I wish more in the gentile Black and white Jewish communities would recognize all he can do.

Then again, I sometimes fear I and others could be instrumentalizing Afro-Jews, kind of giving them a task to save gentile Black and white Jewish conversation from itself! Afro-Jews are stationed in the middle as interlocutors and intermediaries, trying to explain each side to the other.

I do see a definite role for Afro-Jews in that conversation. I'm just wondering, though, Am I instrumentalizing them? Is Rabbi Capers Funnye instrumentalizing them? What's the role that they have to play, if any?

YC: Yeah, absolutely. Yes, he's instrumentalizing them, and that's not a necessarily bad thing. That's exactly what Black and white Christians did in the nineteenth century and early twentieth century when they were figuring out their relationship to each other in the face of hard segregation. And then you have some Black Christians saying, "We're going to have to go our own way. Okay. We cannot get together with y'all."

So here we are in the twenty-first century, and in this particular Black Jewish organization that I guess Funnye is part of, some of them are like, "We really need to bridge this gap." But some of these people are going to say, "We as Black people need to go our own way."

Now, it's really interesting. One of the things I wonder, Why is there a need to bridge these relations? We hear the same conversations within Protestant Christian groups, by the way. "Why are churches segregated?" "Why can't all Black and white religious people get together?"

Well, has anyone bothered to consider why religious segregation emerged in the first place? Did it have to do with the distinct cultural and spiritual innovations that these Black folk created? Of course, the sticking point was Black claims of descent from ancient Hebrews or Israel. So, looking at Black Christianity and Black Judaism, I see that one could make different answers to that question.

JB: So it is instrumentalizing—but a good thing?

YC: So yes, it's instrumentalizing. I can't tell you whether it's a good thing or a bad thing, or whether it will work, but it's part of this larger religion dialogue that we often have in this country. Race is like the big fat elephant in the center of the room when we're having the conversation. Should we just go our own way? Is there one Judaism to which we should all aspire? Of course not.

And then that larger question about "Black-Jewish relations"—I really hate that phrase. It overlooks the asymmetries of power that exist between Blacks and white Jews. I reject the way that these relationships have been framed. My sense is that it seems things are not going well. And so the instrumentalizing part of this work is perhaps in how Funnye sees his role in repairing those relationships. It's a beautiful thing, but I really wish people would see some of these movements in terms of their own self-validating religious ideas and theologies. Because if you understand how and why these ideas are embodied and enacted, it won't be such a surprise when they bubble up to the surface, as with Nick Cannon's comments.

TJ: Please elaborate. In what sense is it not a surprise?

YC: Sometimes these religious beliefs and ideas go in one direction, and it's perfectly fine. And sometimes they go in another direction, and religious folk struggle to defend their identities either because of hostility toward those ideas, as with Cannon's case, or because of skeptics who insist that they are not true or authentic.

And when I say, "It's fine," I'm not making a judgment of whether the beliefs or ideas are good or bad, because it's the normal evolution of religion. So that's all I'll say.

Have you seen Jake Dorman's work on Black Israelite religions?[4] Jake and I have been conversation partners even before the publication of *Black Zion*, and I think he has the most sophisticated take on these issues as any religionist.

JB: I read Professor Dorman's work on Rabbi Wentworth Arthur Matthew and the Commandment Keepers congregation.[5] I really liked his reference to that form of Black Judaism as "bricolage," as something really creative and even meant to be enjoyable and fun.

YC: In Dorman's tremendous book *Chosen People*, I really liked that he centered Black religions, but he's more concerned with questions of race than I am. He thinks there's a fallacy that this Black-Jewish relationship thing is sort of like a harmonious conversation of racialized coequals that might be politically effective. He's skeptical of that project.

As for Black Judaism as a bridge between races, I don't have any feeling about it. I do appreciate the work of our Black rabbis because they really do catch hell. They catch hell from all sides. I don't have any sense of where it's going. I know that I read in newspapers that "the relationship between Blacks and Jews is at an all-time low." I don't know. Does Tiffany Haddish agree with that? Are we talking about religious organizations, are we talking about contemporary social justice movements, or are we talking about personal theologies? I can't speak to that, but if you look at Black religions, all is well. They flourish. This is the way things are.

TJ: Why do you believe Black scholars and writers from the eighteenth and nineteenth centuries focus on what we call the ancient Near East and Judaism? Why not claim Ethiopia or Egypt as a birthplace of civilization? What is it about the Semitic people in particular that people are interested in?

YC: Well, probably I would say it was because of the prominence of the Bible in the Black American imagination even from the earliest period, in slavery, and beyond. So even nineteenth-century Black Christian ministers and scholars—like Edward Blyden, who was enamored with Islam—look at the Bible, and they know that it provides clues to the meaning of Black suffering and cuts to the heart of theodicy. Mainly the Hebrew scriptures tell us there's a chosen people of God called Israelites, but no one says what those chosen people looked like. No one knows what happened to those tribes. So it was almost as if the story was up for grabs.

So I would say again, there was a powerful myth in the story of the Hebrews or the biblical Israelites that really mapped onto so many features of the Black experience from the Diaspora to slavery and beyond. There were so many aspects of that myth that were appealing, and it was readily available to inspire African American religious folk.

JB: What about ancient Egypt? How do you see that figuring in this equation?

YC: Of course, ideas of Africa and Egypt played a part as African American folk created these sacred histories and myths. You see, going back a hundred years now, strands of Islamic orientalism that situated the origins of the Black race in Egypt or the "mystic East." Later on, Black nationalists would do things with the myth of Ethiopian greatness, and Israelite offshoots like Rastafari were created.

So I would say that the myth of the Black Israelites prevailed because the Bible gave great power to the narrative and because this idea was up for grabs. No one really knows who these people were. No one knows what happened after these tribes were scattered. Who are they? What did they become? And that powerful story is still, to this day—it's like, "What happened to the lost tribe? Is that us? Are we one of them?"

If you are a Black Israelite, a Black Muslim, or a Latter-day Saint, you could say that you are descended from those tribes. It's a perfect story. It's a perfect mystery. How do people take religion and plug into it in order to understand ourselves?

And so African Americans are like everyone else: They're plugging into the narratives, and they're creatively finding ways to make the stories real for their circumstances. It is no different from what happens with any other religious people. And that's probably why these ideas are seen as having such power in the present day.

Notes

1. Chireau and Deutsch, *Black Zion*.

2. Chireau, *Black Magic*.
3. Wolfson, "African American Jews," in Chireau and Deutsch, *Black Zion*.
4. Dorman, *Chosen People*.
5. Dorman, "'I Saw You Disappear.'"

7

Talking to American Jews about Whiteness

TJ: Jacques, in 2015 Rabbi Gil Steinlauf wrote a provocative essay in the *Washington Post* with the headline, "Jews in America Struggled for Decades to Become White. Now We Must Give up White Privilege to Fight Racism." The premise is that Jews abandoned their social justice vision as they climbed up the professional, social, and entrepreneurial ranks. Part of the rabbi's argument is that they've chosen to assimilate into white culture instead of leaning on their Jewish identity.

What is your take on the rabbi's essay?

JB: I think the good rabbi was fundamentally correct. He wanted Jewish Americans to "question our whiteness." That's what the consultants like to call "a difficult conversation." Still, a robust percentage of Jews are actually willing to hear what clergy such as Rabbi Steinlauf are saying.

It's something I appreciate about Judaism in this country—the presence of that self-critical column. Not all Jews, obviously, are willing to confront the issue of our white privilege. But many of them are, and that makes us a bit unusual.

TJ: I agree. Theoretically most white Jews would consider your point and ponder through the problem thoughtfully. Though,

I remember talking with Rabbi Gil Steinlauf about whiteness in relation to Jewish identity, and he received a great deal of pushback from his congregants about his *Washington Post* editorial. The criticisms were swift and stinging, emanating from a place of guilt or frustration, maybe both. As far as I could discern from our conversation, Jews seem to be annoyed by the apparent pressure from others to justify their economic and social success. It's as if there's another burden that they are forced to curate, since some or many sit within the top tier of the nation's leading industries.

How do we then actually talk about this in a way that opens up the possibility for real structural and social change?

JB: Good question but first a sidebar: So much of the literature that we read about the history of Blacks and Jews notes that the rabbis (like Rabbi Steinlauf) tended to be *way* out ahead of their congregations in terms of thinking through racial justice issues. I'm thinking, for example, of Clive Webb's *Fight against Fear* and his chapter on southern rabbis in the age of desegregation. The rabbis were the liberals and leftists. The rabbis were the ones reaching out to African American churches. The rabbis were attending the marches. The people in the pews and the board members (oh God, don't get me started on the board members!), for their part, often ignored them or just nodded their heads and avoided the hard truths the rabbis were expounding.

Many clergy in the liberal denominations were pulling the rank and file, as best they could, leftward. Is there a similar dynamic in institutional Black churches?

TJ: No, in fact, it's exactly the opposite!

JB: Seriously?

TJ: Yes. Congregants are constantly challenging ministers and pushing them to become literate in progressive politics, such as on women's issues, for example. The venue for the exchange often happens during midweek meetings, most prominently during Bible studies or retreats for different constituencies in the congregation. In more instances than people are willing to admit, the people in the pews are in fact critically engaging the sermon and selectively choosing what is germane to their individual circumstances. This is especially the case within conservative contexts, where people choose to stay for convenience, familial ties, or tradition but routinely ignore and reject poisonous rhetoric.

> **JB:** So you mean to say that on Black-Jewish issues, the congregants would be more progressive than the minister? Perhaps more inclined to dialogue?

TJ: In many contexts, yes! The congregants set the tone.

Let me give you an example not directly related to Black-Jewish engagement with civil rights—the Montgomery bus boycott. The Dexter Avenue Baptist Church is where Dr. King began his ministry in the 1950s. The congregation identified MLK as the person who would best represent their interests in the public sphere. Even though King's father (Martin Luther King Sr., known as "Daddy" King) and then Morehouse College president Benjamin Elijah Mays tried to dissuade MLK from getting involved in the affairs of the community for fear he would be killed, King rejected their arguments and insisted his congregation had called him for this moment. His example is far more present than our history books have recorded.

To this end, Black congregations have a mind of their own. They can listen to a preacher with whom they totally disagree and still remain active in the church. This, in part, explains why so many African Americans have embraced political commitments and goals that often stand in opposition to church doctrine.

But let's get back to talking about Jewish audiences and their white privilege. Are Jewish audiences ready to confront that?

> **JB:** I think most are, but they'd need African American interlocutors and facilitators, be they Jewish or non-Jewish, to help them think it through. There are two dicey throughlines in Blacks and Jews

discourse: whiteness and Israel. Whiteness is far easier for Jews to discuss than the accusation that they support a genocidal "apartheid state."

My feeling is that Jews in the liberal denominations are receptive to the former discussion. Why? Because many Jews don't feel white or don't feel quite right about being white. Then again, it's hard to frame this conversation with lay people. It's something that Jewish scholars, intellectuals, and clergy think through a great deal, but your physician, nurse, lawyer, venture capitalist, or merchant really hasn't had much of a chance to ponder this.

Having scholars like you visiting synagogues, perhaps with a Jewish scholar in tow, would be a very helpful way of getting audiences to think about whiteness carefully. How would you talk to a liberal Jewish audience about this? What do you want them to understand?

TJ: I guess I would say something like this: "White Jews are given the benefit of the doubt in almost every circumstance. Yes, many gentiles despise your Jewishness, but you nonetheless are the beneficiaries of a social contract that privileges your white body over and against mine. Your whiteness endows you with a ticket to Freedomland.

"So I want you to understand W. E. B. Du Bois's haunting question: 'How does it feel to be a problem?' In far too many instances, when whites see us African Americans, they see a living and embodied problem.

"When I look out into the audience at your synagogue, I see individual faces within a vast sea where individual dynamics, quirks, idiosyncrasies, and so on, are normal and expected. This underscores the stark differences between whiteness and Blackness. Whiteness equates to a vast and endless set of social freedoms. It gives you access to closed doors, and it gives the opportunity to compete in many different publics. And this can be done without any concern for fear, punishment, ostracization from social engagement."

JB: So imagine a congregant at my synagogue comes up to you and says, "Thank you Professor Johnson. You spoke to my heart. How do I change?"

What do you say?

TJ: I don't have an answer. The only way to change is to follow the social justice doctrines that inform Judaism. As an outsider to that tradition, it seems to me that your scriptures are calling you to fight for the "the orphan, the widow and the stranger in your gate" (Deut. 14:29). So I'd suggest you use your own scriptures for your own transformation for how you see Blacks and people of color.

JB: Yeah, here, there is a disconnect. We don't have that relation to scripture, at least not in the liberal denominations. We'd have to work from a resource other than a biblical verse. From my perspective, the fundamental problem is the lack of relationships on the ground.

We all read audiences, Terrence, and sometimes as I am lecturing in a synagogue about white privilege, I'm like, "Man, the Feldmans just aren't feeling me tonight!" I believe the Feldmans are good people, though they're looking at me as if I'm crazy. But we can't give up on the Feldmans. I wish they could speak to an African American mother—Ms. Smith, let's call her—who is worried about her kid jogging through her own mostly white neighborhood or getting pulled over by the police. I mean, sometimes dialogue needs to be organically linked to a real relationship between people. We've talked about the lack of physical proximity and real relationships between Blacks and Jews. That's what makes the Feldmans-Smith meeting so rare, and that is part of the problem.

Recently, you were interviewed by CBS. The segment touched on the question of Jews and whiteness.[1] You texted me that you received tons of responses. What came up?

TJ: African American responses to my CBS interview left me groping for words. In email exchanges, many of them said they were disappointed by the unacknowledged elephant standing in the center of the segment. They perceived the interview failed to address Jewish white privilege and the economic disparities between Blacks and Jews. As far as they were concerned, the current economic and political state of affairs of American Jews foreclosed any possibility of mutually beneficial partnerships. Blacks and Jews are worlds apart from each other.

Other email exchanges and conversations turned in a direction I had not anticipated. African American women in particular engaged me from a point of anguish and brokenness. One woman reminded me of her mother's work as a domestic cleaner in a Jewish family's home. The family was warm and generous to her mother, but she always knew she was "the help."

Another woman shook her head at the Holocaust survivor interviewed in the segment who emphasized that both groups experienced slavery; therefore, he maintained, there was no denying that both groups must work together. She disagreed with that premise. Slavery continues to live in this country, she said. When I ended the conversation, I recalled the time a Jewish woman, a professor at an Ivy League school, told me her nanny was as "strong as a mule."

From what I can gather, Black and white Jewish women's asymmetrical social standings illicit a degree of harm that I don't hear when Black and Jewish men discuss their encounters. What I am hearing captures the underside of Blacks and Jews, the messy psychosocial dimension that can't be easily addressed or pondered. How do we confront the murky, unexplored dimensions of Blacks and white Jews?

JB: I have one suggestion, though it is in the realm of the discursive.

TJ: Okay, go.

JB: Maybe African Americans could ask Jews if they do or don't feel white.

TJ: Okay. Jacques, do you feel white?

JB: Thank you for asking. When thinking about the travails of African Americans in this country, I feel as white as rice, as white as Donald Trump's press secretaries. Police officers ignore me all the time. Shop owners never track my movements to the back of the store. Encounters with security guards are filled with smiles and pleasant banter about sports or the weather. I always get the benefit of the doubt in every professional and economic transaction I engage in. Forgot my wallet? No problem, the coffee is on the house!

TJ: So do you feel white?

JB: No. That's the part I want more Black folks to understand. They don't have to agree with me. I just want them to understand it because a lot of American Jews feel this way.

I don't feel white because I grew up with no cousins or extended family anywhere in the country. It took me decades to realize that was a long-term consequence of most of my father's relatives being murdered in the Holocaust. I don't feel white because when I walk into all-white spaces, I feel like something is really off, like some centuries-long exclusionary logic is being replicated here and that I don't belong anyway. I don't feel white because during those rah-rah American ceremonies, the military processions, and whatnot, something feels off. Internally, there is a monologue raging in my mind that is "cracking wise" about all that whiteness surrounding me. One time I was lecturing at Duke University, and when the golf team walked through the hotel lobby, I couldn't help myself! I suspect—nay, I know—I'm not the only "white" Jew who does this.

I acknowledge the response from a non-Jewish Black person might be, "Cry me a river, Jacques. Your children are not likely to be brutalized by police and a million other quotidian indignities." And that's so true. But it doesn't change the feeling so many Jews have—that we occupy some liminal position.

TJ: Eric Goldstein, in *The Price of Whiteness*, characterized the *whiteness* of Jews in this way: White Jews are consistently the other in many public and professional spaces, even when they occupy seats of power; however, their whiteness guarantees, according to Charles Mills in the *Racial Contract*, that they will benefit from a social contract that protects and privileges whites over Blacks. Unlike African Americans, Goldstein maintains, Jews cannot claim to be marginal or marginalized within a racialized liberalism that rewards European immigrants who reject their ethnic and religious otherness to assimilate into white middle-class America.

JB: Yes, it's a tensile position. We're definitely not marginalized. Liberalism has been so good to the Jews, even though we played no role in its seventeenth- and eighteenth-century origins as a political philosophy! But—and now we're drilling down to our traumas and pathologies—we always fear that we could be marginalized soon! Like the world could fall apart again.

I think with a Jewish audience, it's our job to make the people see ways in which they act "white." Like constantly doing white people stuff and not asking ourselves, "Where's the 14 percent or so of African Americans (in this club, or restaurant, or professional space, or hotel lobby), and why aren't they here?"

TJ: We can't begin to embark upon a rigorous discussion of whiteness until we deal with two critical issues regarding the asymmetrical power relationships between Blacks and white Jews. When Cornel West explores Black-Jewish relationships, he primarily focuses on how white supremacy created the "alliances" that demanded that both groups work to end segregation and legalized racism. Now I'm hearing Black folks from the civil rights generation and the children of the movement express something else: They want to discuss the structures that keep Jews and Blacks apart. In my email exchanges with some of them, whiteness/assimilation and economics are the issues.

JB: How did they correlate those factors with the Jews?

TJ: They don't believe Blacks and Jews can relate to each other or share meaningful encounters until white Jews start a soul-searching journey to explore their rise from immigrants to powerbrokers in two generations.

At times, the email exchanges rehearsed a common and unfortunate narrative of the powerful white Jew, one that essentializes and flattens whiteness. But maybe that's the power and danger of whiteness: It requires the other to essentialize one's identity into one characteristic, yet whiteness is undeniably the trump card that not only affords one access and unearned privileges but also will literally save one's life from unwarranted police shootings.

JB: To call Jews white with no qualifiers attached is counterproductive, but for white Jews to ignore their whiteness is also unhelpful. So, Terrence, if we were working with a Black audience, and we wanted to get the point across that it's complicated to dub Ashkenazi Jews as white, what techniques, exercises, and anecdotes would you recommend?

TJ: It would have to be context specific. How we would address members of a middle-class African Methodist Episcopal church would be different than how we would address BLM organizers.

JB: Tell us first about the AME Church.

TJ: Well, the AME Church is one of the first institutional Black churches to organize in America. It was established in 1787 in Philadelphia. The church, from its origins, required all clergy to receive formal training within institutions of higher learning, and it emphasized economic power, entrepreneurship, and education as the keys to Black freedom. AME ministers had their hands in the NAACP, the National Urban League, Marcus Garvey's United Negro Improvement Association, and the civil rights movement. Alongside this important work, the church established a strong infrastructure that mirrored its public vision. All of this made the members natural allies to established Jews when fighting institutional racism.

JB: So I guess they can draw upon a lot of shared historical work together. What about talking to a mostly younger crowd of BLM activists?

TJ: We'd have to draw upon thinkers, such as Stokely Carmichael, Ella Baker, Angela Davis, and Claudia Jones, many of whom are invoked by BLM activists. The former were informed in part by Du Bois and Anna Julia Cooper, as well as radical left Jewish thinkers who were often Marxist. Carmichael went to high school in New York, and Davis also spent a few years in New York. Carmichael, according to Clayborne Carson, even spoke a little Yiddish!

By appealing to the connection between the radical Left among our Black and Jewish thinkers, we can tap into the transformative aspirations of the Black Lives Matter movement.

JB: When talking about Jewish audiences and their white privilege, I'm thinking about what you said earlier about context. Let's take, for example, ultra-Orthodox Jews. If we gave them a lecture about Jewish white privilege, I think they might respond this way: "Professors, thank you very much for your remarks drawing attention to Jewish white privilege. My concern, however, is this: Every time I walk out onto the streets with my kippah, my black garments, my tallit *katan*, and my long sideburns, I get angry stares, and I occasionally hear antisemitic remarks. People look at me funny. I just don't feel sometimes like I have white privilege especially when I'm being called a 'dirty Jew' or a 'kike.'"

What do we say to them, Terrence? I actually think that they're right. A Reform Jew like me is "passing." But the ultra-Orthodox are not trying to pass.

TJ: Your distinction between Reform and ultra-Orthodox Jews underscores the dire need for us to find in Black and Jewish communities like-minded political and religious groups to speak to each other. This may be the only option left to ignite a wide and far-reaching conversation between two groups that don't see each other as peers. For instance, on the one hand, for BLM members, we really need the radical Left of the Jewish community to address this crowd in an effort to show how they have mutual concerns. On the other hand, for institutional Black churches, we will likely need to revive the Exodus narrative as a motif to galvanize both groups.

JB: Terrence, we are driving toward one of my grand conclusions about Blacks and Jews—that is, both communities are internally wildly heterogenous; thus, there can be no *general* Blacks and Jews dialogue. There can only be dialogues between subgroups in each community. I refer to them as "affinity groups."

BLM has immense support in the Jewish community; that's where the affinities should be sought. In the meantime, maybe we can agree to bracket the question of Israel/Palestine and get to other urgent projects. Maybe from that work there will emerge, almost as a surprise, some answers to the question of Israel/Palestine?

TJ: I agree, or at least I hope so. From what I'm hearing, an increasing number of college-age Jewish Americans have become distressed by Israeli government leaders, such as Benjamin Netanyahu, and want to see an end to the expansion of Israeli settlements in the West Bank. I also suspect they have been embarrassed by Netanyahu's warm relationship with the Trump administration. With this momentum, BLM supporters and a subset of Jewish Americans then might be able to coalesce around Palestinian rights.

Note

1. Johnson interview by Duncan, "Holocaust Survivor."

8

The Loop and Minister Farrakhan

JB: How many times in our study of African American–Jewish American relations in the United States have we encountered a phenomenon we call the loop? First, let's explain it to our readers. It starts, usually, when a figure in the Black community makes a disparaging remark about Jews. Then . . .

TJ: Prominent Jewish leaders ask well-known and prominent African American leaders to make a public statement denouncing the antisemitic comment by that random Black individual . . .

JB: Meanwhile, many Jewish organizations, leaders, journalists, and so on, kick into overdrive, and the disparaging remark assumes the status of a national security issue . . .

TJ: Within minutes of the alleged verbal assault, a "representative Black" speaks on behalf of the "Black community" to forcefully denounce Black antisemitism, signaling the community's unremitting support of Jews.

JB: The "representative Black" is lambasted by some other Blacks but held up as a model of civility, civil rights (and Blackness) by Jews.

TJ: This narrative plays out in almost every major city where there's a significant Jewish and Black population. In fact, as long as the antisemitic remark is articulated anywhere within the contiguous

United States, Blacks are expected to say something, anything, that rejects the person's insidious beliefs.

JB: Perhaps no one person has spun more loops than Minister Louis Farrakhan, leader of the Nation of Islam. His copious antisemitic diatribes in the 1980s and 1990s—for example, "Judaism is a gutter religion," "Jews are responsible for the ships that brought our forefathers to slavery," "Hitler was an evil genius," and more—are known to all and sundry, and we needn't rehearse them here. Perhaps everything that can be said—or screamed—about this subject has been said. I feel it's time to approach this topic a little differently.

TJ: I can't wrap my mind around Minister Louis Farrakhan and the Jewish community's responses to his speeches. Whenever Minister Farrakhan opens his mouth, white Jews always seem to be within arm's reach, clinging to his every word for confirmation of what they already suspect or know from previous speeches. And he never fails to deliver! And their outcries legitimate him and wrongly weaponize his hyperbolic rhetoric regarding Judaism. Jews fail to interrogate Minister Farrakhan on his own terms.

JB: Okay, tell us about those terms.

TJ: He's informed by Black preaching, and its performative element is designed to incite, probe, and trouble the waters before offering scripture's answer to the problem at hand. If you listen to his characterizations of African Americans, especially during the 1980s and 1990s, his tone and indictment of single mothers and the men who abandon them are piercing and pernicious to an unfamiliar ear. I don't need to justify or explain his political and theological views on Israel or Judaism. I'm not a member of the Nation of Islam, nor do I contribute to it. But at the height of Minister Farrakhan's popularity in the 1990s, college-age and working-class African Americans, mostly men, embraced his acute and astounding rhetorical renunciations of white supremacy as well as his profound appeal for Black self-love and the restoration of two-parent households. Many of us were excited to hear the clarity of his vision for Black people, but we ignored his attacks against Jews and Judaism because the comments didn't fit into the blueprint for our individual and collective freedom.

Our critical engagement with his speech is reflective of how many religious practitioners pick and choose what they will accept from their spiritual guides. Some would call this "Black listening," an extension of the African American call-and-response tradition that informs the dialogical encounter within Black sacred spaces. Without the backdrop of the performative dimension of African American religions, you can't sufficiently interpret the exchange between Black religious leaders and their audience.

JB: So I have three quick-hit responses. First, when I was writing a book that touched on Afrocentrism, I used to attend a lot of Afrocentric rallies, and I noticed precisely what you were saying.[1] (Naturally there's a difference between Afrocentrism and the Nation of Islam's worldview.) The events were self-consciously hyperbolic. It was kind of joyous—cathartic, actually—and often really funny, with the speakers just pillorying their audiences (and others) and eliciting waves of laughter. So I see what you are saying about the performative element.

Second, I have never once felt a desire to ask an African American friend or colleague to repudiate something that Farrakhan says.

TJ: And why is that?

JB: Because I don't see how the two are connected. If I am spending time with a person, I don't assume he or she has an issue with Jews.

Third, I just can't stand the things Farrakhan says about Jews and others.

Now a question: Do you think an insult that some Blacks feel when they are asked to "renounce" Farrakhan is that they are being asked to distance themselves from a person whose only similarity to them is phenotypical?

TJ: It is insulting and degrading, and it reflects the unacknowledged paternalism that creeps its ugly head at different points in the long and oftentimes combative encounters between Blacks and Jews in America. As long as Jews see themselves as donors rather than allies who stand in solidarity with Blacks, the relationship between Blacks and Jews will remain unequal, paternalistic, and unknowingly self-serving. The political demands in exchange for Jewish financial support equate, unfortunately, to what a bondsman requires of his or her underlings.

JB: Yes, this inequality is at the root of the problem. I'm with you on that, all the way. But then we have to get to the sentiments expressed and their prevalence. In having this discussion, my role model is Barbara K. Smith, who started her important piece with the claim "I am anti-Semitic."[2] I never thought she was. But I appreciated what she was doing. She was starting the conversation in a very different place, a more authentic place. I think Smith was really onto something, starting a conversation from a place of authenticity.

Do you think this would be helpful in Blacks and Jews dialogue and serve as a way of getting past the latest Farrakhan remark?

TJ: I agree with you. Starting at a level of authenticity is necessary for healing the deep wounds and addressing the unwitting insults made and harms done to each other.

How do we push beyond the impasse between Blacks and Jews? Authenticity is demanded and required. But the cultural moment makes it almost impossible to create the conditions for it to happen. What will we gain from authentic talk? What would it look like?

Authenticity assumes we are all entering the conversation on equal grounds or in possession of power. We may have to bracket our desire for authenticity until we figure out how to implement justice and reparations to restore what has been systematically stolen or denied to African Americans.

How do we discuss Jewish racism without getting slapped with charges of antisemitism?

JB: Well, this is intriguing. You've deconstructed "authenticity" itself as a sort of ruse. Authenticity is inauthentic. I still believe in the category, by the way, because I meet authentic people here and there—and if I didn't, I'd completely lose hope. But let's follow your logic and answer your questions as authentically as I can.

I'll start with Jewish racism. In the last couple of months, my preparations for this book led me to much more intensive reading of scholarly monographs and articles. And I must say, what I found troubled me. I was troubled that I had to recalibrate an equation I had often worked with. The original equation went like this: The overwhelming majority of Jews were averse to white supremacy, were allies to their African American brothers and sisters, and were willing participants in the civil rights struggle. What has happened in the last few months is I have recalibrated my percentages. I am finding more evidence that the heroic Jews, who I believed were in the majority, were in the minority. However, as I looked around, I realized that the very existence of this minority among whites and white-ethnics *was in itself very unusual*—which is to say, what's unusual about Jews is that a small percentage engage in all the decent behaviors I mentioned previously.

So to answer your question of how do we discuss Jewish racism without getting slapped with the charge of antisemitism, it is by having Jews, like me and so many others, identify this as a problem. Being self-critical is how dialogue gets done.

> **TJ:** Why do you assume Jews have a certain role to play in freedom struggles? Does it have anything to do with Jewish identity as a "chosen people"?

JB: No, not at all. It has to do with their history of being the victims of discrimination and abusive state and non-state power. It's a claim made from empirical observation, not theology.

> **TJ:** The subtext of your argument is noteworthy. Are you suggesting that the Torah's theology of social justice is the missing element

in Jewish education? Unfortunately, what you've uncovered is that to sustain the American dream and tradition of exceptionalism, we have to maintain these myths about who we are collectively. On the one hand, as a Jewish American, you must tell yourself that Judaism requires that you stand in solidarity with African Americans and fight for their social justice. On the other hand, I need to find any and all evidence that America and American democracy will work someday for more than the roughly 30 percent of African Americans who are in the middle class. If I don't carry this faith, I risk falling into the trap that Cornel West calls deep "nihilism" in *Race Matters.*

Interestingly enough, you are calling attention to what BLM has been raising for five to six years—that is, this country was not designed for us.

JB: Well, one place to look for the evidence of Jewish support for BLM's social justice goals is in that cohort of Jews that are impassioned by these issues. Naturally, there are others. I agree that those who want to make American democracy work for all might be in the minority, but their very existence should be a solvent of nihilism.

Okay, we've talked about one half of the loop; now let's get to the other. Adolph Reed, a writer I really enjoy reading, argues there is no such thing as Black antisemitism. He never denies there are individual antisemites, but he does not believe there is a paradigm or any culture or tradition of Black antisemitism.[3]

TJ: Professor Reed's point is substantial. The classic literature on Black politics in the early and mid-twentieth century overwhelmingly focuses on themes ranging from integration, nationalisms, and self-help to economic independence, human rights, and reparations. The competing agendas overlap on one particular issue—an agreement on what constitutes systemic and structural racism. Antisemitism is not intrinsic within the development of Black political thought.

Does antisemitism exist in Black communities? Of course.

JB: Here I want to qualify that a bit. If you look at what Jews prior to the 1980s were complaining about in their encounters with African Americans, it was a kind of quotidian antisemitism. It was very local and kind of banal. It was a little bit of the "Christ killer" stuff, a little bit of the "cheap Jew" and the "exploitative Jew." That type of stuff happens when communities are living close together under conditions of inequality, and it was not specific to African Americans. To me, that wasn't a worry.

What happened in the 1980s and 1990s, however, changes the game a little bit with the publication of *The Secret Relationship between Blacks and Jews* by the Nation of Islam. Why? Because a *paradigm* emerges, a go-to, a resource where some folks can access ready-built theories of antisemitism. And these things keep coming up.

So in terms of things that concern me, I want to say that the former episodes of low-level antisemitic remarks certainly didn't make me happy, but I never thought of this antisemitism as a uniquely Black thing. I didn't think it had established a foothold in the African American community.

The persistence of certain tropes about Jews in certain sectors of the African American community does concern me. It worries me much less than white supremacist rhetoric, but its presence is still a concern.

TJ: I disagree. You're embellishing the degree to which African Americans caricature Jews. The tropes to which you are referring are deeply rooted in *American* culture and white Christianity. The media and American Jewish leaders give Farrakhan far too much attention. In many ways, they fetishize this guy.

When college-age Black students come to me to discuss the state of affairs of Black leadership, they don't mention Minister Farrakhan or the Nation of Islam. For Generation Z, he's embraced as a grandfatherly figure, meaning he's respected but not referenced by BLM activists while figures such as Frantz Fanon, Ella Baker, Malcolm X, and Angela Davis are.

Here's my bigger concern: The media and white Jews keep digging up offensive quotes from the minister instead of focusing on the leaders and activists who are willing to work with them. White Jewish leaders, most of whom are from the civil rights generation, cannot keep referring to Minister Farrakhan as if his views are representative of an entire people.

JB: I think you're correct about the disproportionate amount of attention that his every utterance about the Jews and Israel receives. There's no doubt about that. My concern is that they have been established as a paradigm. As students of the history of antisemitism know, once these paradigms emerge, they're virtually impossible to eradicate.

TJ: But when do Jews call out Jewish anti-Black racism? When *The Bell Curve* was published in 1994, during the height of the tense arguments between Minister Farrakhan and Jewish leaders, I don't recall many Jews calling out the book for the racist backdrop that framed the book's argument—namely, that Blacks are intellectually inferior to whites.

Do test scores equate to *natural* intelligence?

JB: No. Most Jews were decidedly not happy with *The Bell Curve* and that whole neo-conservative jamboree. Jews from Noam Chomsky to Stephen Jay Gould, and countless others, did criticize it. *The Bell Curve* harked back to racial science and policy prescriptions linked to state biopower that freaked most Jews out (having run afoul of those things themselves).[4]

I think you have in mind the Jewish reluctance to *censor* the book. Jews tend to get very nervous about censorship, seeing as how we think that censorship leads to even worse outcomes. What complexifies matters is that these neo-conservative ideas were backed by think tanks and donors who gave it salience beyond its actual scientific value. *The Bell Curve* had this massive "scientific" scaffolding about it. My view is that the American research university is built to invalidate that sort of stuff. Many Jews wanted the university to do just that, as opposed to censoring the text; that would just give it more prominence. Then again, in the digital age, I find myself rethinking my hard First Amendment positions of yore.

In any case, as educators, it's our job to talk through these issues with our students and to apprise them of the pointlessness, the immorality, and the idiocy of racist and antisemitic worldviews. We spoke of authenticity as one mode of doing this, though you seemed skeptical of authenticity's authenticity. What else can we do as professors to engage this issue in our classrooms?

TJ: I don't think there's one way to address this issue. My preference is to address it by beginning with fragility, which is by far very dangerous and counterproductive within our current context, which is inundated with debates on censorship and free speech on college campuses. But I'm reminded of my time in Morehouse College, where the presumption was that we came to college to be restored—if not transformed—to begin the long and arduous process of finding and building our intellectual voice. One way to do so is to begin with the notion that we are fragile, and this is interesting for Blacks and Jews because we enter places already as broken vessels. We are finding ways to grow back what has been torn asunder, but we're stuck. We're at a loss because no one wants to admit that they need to be rebuilt.

Jacques, moving forward, in our course how do you envision addressing concerns related to political disagreements in our segregated publics, where truth is regulated by the norms of one's political party, religious commitments, and racial politics?

JB: As for being "stuck" or "broken," the thing I have always sensed, and always admired, about the African American church is its sense of hopefulness in spite of it all. "Even so, come Lord Jesus"—that sort of thing. I'm going to need a massive infusion of that hopefulness as an antidote to the way I feel today, in late 2020.

All we can do going forward, my colleague, is give our students all the great scholarship to read, have them encounter all that sublime art, and keep modeling dialogue, admitting errors, self-correcting.

It's *our* standard of decency. As a professor of Chinese literature once taught me, it's not that a standard of decency prevails—it usually doesn't—but a standard of decency must always *exist*.

Notes

1. Berlinerblau, *Heresy in the University*.
2. Barbara Smith, "Between a Rock," in Adams and Bracey, *Strangers and Neighbors*, 766.
3. Reed, "What Color Is Anti-Semitism?," in Adams and Bracey, 24–26.
4. Herrnstein and Murray, *Bell Curve*.

9

Secularism and Mr. Kicks

TJ: Jacques, tell me what you mean by "secularism." I grew up in a middle-class conservative Black church that decried secularism as evil and something only white folks believed in and practiced. Even as a kid, however, I found the church's perspective a bit odd, as all the adults in my family and neighborhood went to juke joints and clubs, and drank alcohol—all of which were linked to "secular" behavior—the night before Sunday morning services. That being said, the narrative of secularism as opposing religion and reflecting the values of white folks remains operative in many Black communities.

JB: As a person who has studied, taught, and written about secularism for decades, I am saddened but not surprised. I think of the work of one scholar who recently wrote, "Whiteness is secular, and the secular is White."[1] I understand the point but strongly disagree. In my own research, I often note that secularism is the most misunderstood ism in the American, even global, political lexicon.

But before I offer you a definition, there's something I'm curious about. People in your church associated secularism with juke joints, clubs, and alcohol? Did you ever hear that Oscar Brown Jr. song "Mr. Kicks"? Do you mean to say that people in your congregation correlated the secular with the demonic, with Mr. Kicks?

TJ: Yes. Secularism is demonic, not of God within my hometown's small Baptist church setting. But there's a twist to the story. The church community recognized that most of the members—some more than others—would dabble in the secular. But as long as you embraced the Sabbath by finding your way back to a Sunday service—regardless of how often you partied, smoked, and so forth—members of the church would look the other way.

Of course, academics such as Vincent Lloyd, whom you quoted earlier, locate Black secularism as a kind of hermeneutical lens through which Black religion comprehends existence, nature, history, and so on. And instead of relying on theological language, Black secularism turns to politics and culture to decode the problem at hand. As you can see, his definition maintains the liminal "divide" between religion and secularism that was operative in my childhood church.

JB: Gosh, I always claimed that secularism had an image problem.

Okay, for starters the definition the people in your church invoked is not incorrect, but it's not one that political scientists would use. The church folks and many, many others are defining secularism in terms of a "lifestyle." That lifestyle is inflected with godlessness, sexual deviance, creaturely excess, and more. This is why your church brothers and sisters are not wrong in equating secularism with nonbelief. From the moment the term "secularism" was coined in 1851 by George Jacob Holyoake, it was immediately confused with atheism.

I also hear a little Augustine in what you just mentioned about Sunday morning worship versus Saturday night partying. In this I hear overtones of the earthly and the godly kingdom. Were your church brethren saying that here on Earth we do silly, creaturely things (on Saturday night); then, when we go to church (on Sunday), we are, like, in an annex of God's city?

TJ: No. It's a strange phenomenon. They characterized the blues or hip hop as the devil's music, for example, even though many of them regularly listened to and sometimes pursued careers in secular music. With this in mind, they desperately wanted to develop traditions and cultural habits that would distinguish themselves from the white world and to find safety within settings and practices hidden from the purview of the white normative gaze. Secular music was a by-product of their condemnation of the world, and at the same time, the music was deeply indebted to Negro spiritual and gospel music. Many of the churchgoers who criticized secular music found themselves deeply ingrained in and indebted to the practices the church deemed to be worldly and in opposition to God's divine commandments, the so-called secular. For instance, they sought the advice of a tarot card reader or consulted a diviner to cure a sickness or to impede a spouse from pursuing extramarital affairs.

If outsiders could experience the nuanced theological practices and beliefs within historic Black religious settings, we would have a far richer understanding of Black life and our enduring spirituality. We would also come to accept that the tension between the secular and the sacred, especially within Black church settings, was far more rhetorical than substantive.

JB: Having a day apart from "the normative white gaze"—that's a non-secular day, according to you?

TJ: Yes. The day symbolized a return to spaces and communities where people felt safe, welcomed, and wanted; and where cultural norms, values, and practices were second nature; and where no one needed a translator to know what was happening.

I have vivid memories of my grandmother's neighbors driving or walking to their spaces of worship. Some put on their finest clothes Saturday morning for worship with the Seventh-day Adventist congregation. Early risers on Sunday were generally headed to a mainline Baptist or AME church. Those leaving their homes later in the day, maybe at noon, were either members of the Sanctified Church, Pentecostals, or the Church of God in Christ; or they belonged to the Nation of Islam. I imagine in most of these spaces, a good number of people would have preferred going to a baseball game or a park, or remaining in bed. But there was a restorative element in mostly Black religious settings, and what we invented and walked away with provided resources for when we left "the veil" and returned to a world that looked upon us with contempt and disgust.

JB: So in your community, the secular world was the white world?

TJ: Yes, the secular was white.

JB: Now we need to insert this into a Blacks and Jews framework. As you know, Jews are often associated with the secular. In my book *How to Be Secular*, I talk about how hard Jews "leaned in" to secularism, which they defined not as an anti-metaphysical doctrine but as a separation of church and state, in the 1950s and 1960s.[2] The term "secular Jew" has a salience and normalcy that is unmatched. For instance, how often do you hear "secular Muslim" or "secular Evangelical"? You don't, but "secular Jew" has a familiar ring to it.

What about a "secular African American"? Can you describe a few qualities associated with such a person and what his or her standing in the community might be?

TJ: The secular African American—and I must reiterate I'm not a fan of the category—is someone who does not acknowledge God or rejects Black religion.

Until the last decade or so, popular Black musicians would almost always thank God or acknowledge their upbringing in a religious community whenever they accepted an award. Communities expected artists and entertainers, regardless of the homophobic or sexist rants in their music, to join in the ritual of publicly acknowledging the "invisible" or background sources of their success, especially at the Grammy Awards ceremony. This symbolic gesture signaled to Black audience members they were members of the "tribe." This gave the musicians a pass or a "get-out-of-jail-free" card when they would inevitably get into trouble and would need Blacks to support them. The public gestures also reinforced our humanity, despite what white folks thought of us.

Is there an equivalent in the Jewish community?

JB: What a question! It sort of breaks things wide open for us analytically.

No, there is no comparable get-out-of-jail-free card for Jews. A Jewish American who runs afoul of the law can't claim his or her love of the God of Israel as a way of winning back the favor of most Jews. Maybe that's because so many secular Jews are deeply suspicious of that move; they see it as a white evangelical ruse à la Chuck Colson or Roger Stone—that sort of thing. You know, maybe an incriminated Jew could claim to be a staunch supporter of Israel and point out that he wrote huge checks to the Jewish Federation. But notice that the Jews who have gotten into trouble—I mean, *big* trouble—such as Bernie Madoff, Jeffrey Epstein, and Harvey Weinstein never "found God," as it were. There were no yarmulkes and whatnot at their bail hearings. All Weinstein had was that little walker with the tennis-ball feet he schlepped into the courtroom.

I'm really intrigued by your question. It makes me see there is no "fore and aft" Saturday-to-Sunday (or Friday-to-Saturday) shift between sin and godliness for most American Jews.

But a little sidebar: Acknowledging that neither of us would invoke "secular African American" as a term of disrespect, can you name some secular African Americans? You'll see why I'm asking in a moment. Who are they, and why are they considered secular?

TJ: I don't particularly like the term "secular." I prefer the category of "humanist."

Folks such as Jean Toomer, Alice Walker, Audre Lorde, William R. Jones, and Anthony Pinn, to name a few, explore the religious and ethical dimensions of what I've called elsewhere "sacred subjectivity" without relying on any theistic claims; yet, to some extent, they all acknowledge an ongoing mystery or sacredness within Black life as it relates to the tragic nature of anti-Blackness. In other words, human flourishing emerges as a fundamental pillar underscoring many of the emancipatory goals of Black freedom struggles. To this end, liberation, or freedom, almost always begins with the choices that individuals pursue, not with God's hand intervening in history.

Political rights are secondary to achieving embodied freedom. Why is this the case? The state is often conflicted when the "Negro problem" surfaces vis-à-vis legal battles to end slavery, segregation, and police violence, for instance; so Blacks, in turn, envision the state's retreat as a symbol of the limits of liberalism and democracy, both of which decry aspects of the secular.

Here's what I'm trying to say: The perceived inhumanity of African Americans dates back to Christianity's entanglement with colonialism. I don't believe we can embrace the secular until we've fully deconstructed Christianity's role in building the empire and in anti-Blackness. Do you understand my point?

JB: I do understand it, and I'm focusing on what you just said about Christianity. I'm starting to develop a point. It's coming, it's percolating. Give me a minute.

TJ: As you said, secularism has a public relations problem. What is missing in secularism is the acknowledgment of the interior life. Black interior life is so important.

Does secularism account for an interiority that can be retrieved in an emancipatory project?

JB: There are a couple of things to address here. When I was studying secularism, I always found it amazing that critics would assume it was a totalizing worldview, something as broad and well thought out as Christianity or Islam. The truth of the matter is that secularism is a subproject of liberalism and has a very particular beat. Its job is to regulate relationships between governments and religious groups, and between religious groups themselves. It's a big job, but that's all that political secularism is supposed to do. It's dry and legalistic. Secularism is, actually, quite boring. Yet Fundamentalists (alongside a bazillion postcolonial theorists) rebranded it as a multi-headed dragon spitting hellfire on your "belief in God."

What's so interesting about our discussion is that you are constructing—and it's not incorrect—secularism as a lifestyle-metaphysical choice, whereas many scholars see it as a narrow political doctrine focused on church/mosque/ashram/synagogue–state relations. Secularism is like a referee. It's not cool enough or capacious enough to get into people's interiority.

TJ: So you point out a conundrum within Black political thought—that is, historically African Americans have not had to battle the church-state distinction because they have been far too focused on obtaining rights and equal access, and on ending political and economic barriers. Because anti-Blackness is a kind of ontology at the heart of our social dilemma, secularism has not been in the wheelhouse of Black politics due to its deracialized position. It has not been in anything.

JB: Are you saying African Americans have not had the relative luxury of caring about church-state issues because there are so many other injustices to attend to? If so, recall that in the mid-twentieth century, church-state issues were of central concern to major Jewish organizations. No longer is that the case, but this comparison gets to the core of some of the differences between white Jews and Blacks in this country: The former were deeply invested in secularism—understood as the separation of church and state—which is a subproject of liberalism, whereas Blacks seem either to discount it or to dislike it.

TJ: A number of factors prevented Blacks from diving into the religious freedom debate, most of which had to do with securing emancipation for slavery. In subsequent years, I think the debate took a back seat to securing voting rights, access to housing, and viable public school options.

Keep in mind that Blacks were not (at least historically) persecuted for their religious orientation. They faced violence and death because of their skin color.

As a secularist, how do you come to terms with the comprehensive nature of anti-Blackness?

JB: Hey, Terrence, now I know what you unlocked in me earlier when you mentioned Christianity and secularism's role in anti-Blackness.

If you look at the history of the American secular movement, you will quickly notice that it has one recurring enemy—white conservative Christianity. Look at the figure of Robert Ingersoll, who advocated for what was known as the "Nine Demands of Liberalism" in 1872. The group's plank was separationist, and its members were especially excised by others who wanted to add a preamble to the Constitution that referred to Jesus Christ. American secularists have been battling this cohort—a cohort with implicit and explicit links to white supremacist worldviews—for 150 years. From the Scopes trial (1924), to *Engel v. Vitale* (1962), to school voucher programs (beginning in 1989), secular Americans have been engaged in a pitched battle with precisely the same group that has made life for Blacks so difficult.

I acknowledge and lament that American secular movements have been overwhelmingly white. And if we actually had more histories of them, we'd find racists in their ranks, for sure. Then again, these movements and African Americans share a common enemy! But why have African Americans, who are very pragmatic voters, not sought alliances with American secularists?

TJ: What you have outlined is a fragment of a bigger problem in American society: White conservative Christianity is woven throughout our federal and state governments. So I'm not sure how this effort in any way helps or extends Black politics. Inserting the name of Jesus is not the issue; the issue is really centered on voting rights. Can felons have the right to vote? There are also issues around reproductive rights. Those are the issues that folks are grappling with—issues that are linked to secularism but are not substantively secularist.

Richard Wright provides an interesting counterpoint to my claim.[3] He is ripped apart and rejected by his community for his strikingly secular political ideologies and the rejection of liberalism. Remember, the elite literary community pitted Wright against Baldwin, the darling of the liberal New York writers' circle, and Wright seemed to feel he was rejected because he didn't buy into the narrative that Blacks could redeem anti-Black and anti-working-class society.

JB: That rejection might have to do with Wright's communist dalliance, no? Something I notice in a lot of the scholarly literature on Blacks and Jews is that in the mid-twentieth century, communists scared the crud out of mainstream African Americans and Jewish Americans. Both were deeply concerned about Reds within their own ranks. Jews had the Rosenberg trials, some crazy percentage of the membership of Communist Party of the United States of America, and all those types Joel Coen and Ethan Coen spoofed in their underappreciated film *Hail, Caesar!* Blacks had activists such as Paul Robeson and Claudia Jones, as well as intellectuals who came and went such as Langston Hughes, Ralph Ellison, Chester Himes, and so on.

Terrence, do you think that secularism in the African American consciousness assumes a similar place that communism did?

TJ: That's a great insight, but I don't think so. Robin D. G. Kelley has written extensively on African American communists in the South and their expansive reach within Black communities.[4] In fact, it was common to find Black ministers either directly involved or working in the background to ensure the safety and longevity of communists and other groups that wanted to secure freedom and justice for African Americans. Robeson and Jones, for instance, are remembered as radical leftists who fought for Black freedom.

As far as I can tell, Blacks don't reject secularism because it's radical; they do so based on prior traditions and customs that don't embrace a secular-religious divide. For a case in point, historically, folks such as Malcolm X, Ella Baker, Minister Louis Farrakhan, and Angela Davis could speak in a Black church or religious setting without any contempt from the audience. Why? I think it's because their love for the people was religiously sufficient for them. The audience members didn't care if those folks believed in God or no. What mattered was whether the speaker unabashedly loved Black folks or not.

JB: Terrence, if you were kind enough to arrange an invitation for me to speak to a group at your church and try to make the case for secularism to them, what advice would you give me the night before I made my appeal?

TJ: Don't talk about secularism. Talk about jazz, which you also know something about. As soon as you even whisper the word "secularism," people will close their ears and tune you out.

Notes

1. Lloyd, "Introduction," in Kahn and Lloyd, *Race and Secularism*, 5.
2. Berlinerblau, *How to Be Secular*.
3. Wright, *Uncle Tom's Children*.
4. See Kelley's *Hammer and Hoe*.

10

Israel/Palestine

TJ: There appears to be a public code of silence among college-age Jews concerning Israel's treatment of Palestinians. I hear rumblings of young American Jews criticizing Israel within their inner circles, but that criticism fails to see the light of day in broader classroom discussions. They seem to want to protect the memory of Israel's historic role and meaning within Judaism at the expense of shedding light on the plight of Palestinians.

Is this a fair reading? What does this anxiety among college-age Jews mean for Israel's political future?

JB: There's a real issue here. The "code of silence" is not necessarily pure hype. I think, though, that it's more of a reflex than a coordinated plan. Jews have been conditioned not to talk about Israel in non-Jewish spaces, unless those spaces are full of evangelical Christians (spaces where many young Jews are not).

You are right, though. Young Jewish Americans are reluctant to be critical of Israel in our classroom, and our classroom has always been a pretty open and accommodating space. Imagine them in other classrooms!

What do you wish they would say or reflect on? Also, why do you think they adhere to this code of silence, which I acknowledge has a basis in reality?

TJ: Before I discuss the general code of silence that we all fall prey to within our respective communities, I want you to elaborate on the current state of affairs in Israel. Specifically, I want you to help me understand the development and the consequences of the growing discontent among young American Jews with Israel's expanding settlements in the West Bank and with Prime Minister Benjamin Netanyahu's cozy relationship with our racist former commander in chief Donald J. Trump.

> **JB:** Let me speak in broad sociological terms. On every college campus, such as our own, you'll find four categories of Jews vis-à-vis the state of Israel. The first really has no strong thoughts on the issue either way. The second is hard left and veers toward anti-Zionist positions (which are relatively small in number). The third, and much larger, comprises center-right and right-wing Jews who are reflexively supportive of the Jewish state no matter what it does. They used to be centrists but are now veering to Trumpism. The fourth, and the largest, cohort on a campus such as our own represents the liberal and progressive Jews. Terrence, as you surmise, these latter students experience real internal tension and frustration.

TJ: Why does that frustration exist?

> **JB:** Because these kids are beholden to all sorts of center, center-left, and left-wing worldviews on every imaginable policy issue in the United States. They are deeply opposed to classic conservative and/or Republican policies, and their opposition aligns them almost perfectly politically with most of their African American classmates.
>   LGBTQ rights? Check.
>   Reproductive freedoms? Check.
>   Protecting the environment? Check.
>   Income equality? Check.
>   Anti-racism? Check.
>   Then comes Israel with a prime minister who essentially mocked President Barack Obama and extended a warm, complicit embrace to his successor, President Trump. The hard-right politics of the Jewish state places these young people in an incredibly difficult political position. Our students have been stuck there for about two decades.

They abhor the right-wing government of Israel, but for Jews the very existence of Israel is inextricably bound to their own existence in the Diaspora.

TJ: And does this come at the expense of Palestinians?

JB: It comes at the expense of publicly calling out the Israeli government and doing honest activist work. I will grant you that.

TJ: The point brings us back to your earlier argument: We all adhere to varying codes of silence. Some African Americans are guilty of ignoring homophobia, transphobia, and sexism within institutionalized religions. But we don't generally ostracize or limit resources to organizations that hold religious or political doctrines contrary to our own. We find other ways to express our disdain. Not the case with Israel. Any perceived and real verbal assault against the country will be met with fierce and substantial pushback.

Do you want to risk another generation of potential partnerships because American Jews refuse—at least publicly—to grapple with BLM's advocacy of Palestinian rights? If young Jewish Americans plan to remain allies with progressive Black political organizations such as Black Lives Matter, they will need either to agree to disagree with the group's criticisms of Israeli settlements, for instance, in Palestinian land or to stand in solidarity with BLM's political position. I don't expect young Jewish Americans to disavow Israel wholeheartedly, but I do expect a critical engagement with its policies and practices toward Palestinians and Afro-Jews, for that matter. I am hearing that this is already happening within Jewish families and leftist Jewish groups.

Having said that, Jewish organizations maintain a high bar when it comes to African American criticisms of Israel. In fact, when Minister Louis Farrakhan was at the height of his popularity in the 1980s and 1990s and singled out Jews as the source for Black subjugation and condemned Israel for dehumanizing Palestinians, every known Black leader was expected to repudiate him or face from their Jewish supporters a stiff penalty in the form of withholding financial support from leading African American institutions.

JB: We have spoken about Minister Farrakhan previously. In brief, though, if all he made were "Israel" comments, the Jewish community would probably never have noticed him.

As for BLM, I don't disagree with what you're saying. In fact, if I were some type of consultant to American Judaism, I would advise adherents as follows: Start dialoguing immediately with people in the BLM movement because they're going to be around for a while, and they're probably going to constitute a future leadership class in the United States. But here is a complicating factor: These liberal Jewish kids who are loath to criticize Israel in our class will likely *unload* on the Netanyahu government in Jewish settings, exactly as you noted.

You once told the class—namely, the non–African American portion of the class—that the Black church is an open discursive space where incredibly diverse opinions are expressed, often quite forthrightly (as long as white people aren't around). Conversely, what Blacks might say in a mixed audience might be a bit more diplomatic. It's a double standard, I admit, but why can't Jews live by that double standard as well? That is to say, at the dinner table and at their synagogues, jawing with their parents and rabbis, they are very critical of the Israeli government. Externally, however, for reasons I'll get into in a moment, they are quiet and timid.

TJ: Jacques, the stakes are very different. If you sign a boycott, divestment, and sanctions (BDS) petition or criticize Israel, from my experience, you are labeled anti-Semitic. The message is clear: Israel is off-limits to non-Jews and especially to African Americans. All of this stops the conversation and prevents any kind of dialogue between African American progressive groups such as BLM and Jewish groups such as the Jewish Federation.

JB: First things first. The two positions, as you know, aren't precisely the same. Anti-Zionism is not a synonym for antisemitism, but I understand where you're coming from. Being critical of Israel is not going to earn you the antisemitic label nowadays if the critique is not couched in an oratorical tradition, which I'll argue in a moment owes its existence to the discursive genius of Black Power intellectuals. There are ways of criticizing Israel that are constructive, and there are ways that are so unyieldingly one-sided that they obviate discourse.

However, you're absolutely right. A BDS petition does trigger very, *very* extreme responses from Jewish kids who support the state of Israel. For whatever reasons, Terrence, among Jews exists a type of epigenetic posttraumatic stress disorder, whereby someone's signing some piece of paper encouraging a boycott and divestment of Israel unleashes a very extreme reaction in many Jewish hearts and minds. Do we overreact? Yeah, I think that we overreact.

Here's what's interesting: Jews expect African Americans to have a similar epigenetic response to certain types of code words, policy initiatives, and so forth. We really do understand that because we have similar experiences of entire civilizations collapsing on top of us. It's curious to me that there isn't greater understanding by some African Americans for a typically Jewish reaction that might not, admittedly, be totally rational.

TJ: Here's one point to keep in mind: African Americans don't have the political and economic power to punish white racists in the academy, white supremacists who live within arm's reach of our communities, or whites who verbally assault us.

To a degree, you are correct. African Americans should have an instinctual response to violent signs and symbols. But you may not like my response: We respond by inventing languages and adopting political strategies to survive violent reactions in our quest to become rights-bearing citizens.

Unfortunately, the ongoing debate around Israel and Palestine has created an unnecessary wall between many progressive African Americans and like-minded white Jews. In fact, I recently spoke with an African American colleague about this topic. Her response: "I would never risk my job by entering the Israeli-Palestinian debate. I support Israel's right to exist, but there's no way I could enter the debate without acknowledging the Palestinians' abuse by the Israeli government. That alone would end my career. I'm sorry, but it's not worth it."

JB: Your colleague was a tenured professor, I take it.

TJ: Yes! And she supports the state of Israel! The political consequences faced by Black activists such as Alice Walker and Angela Davis—both of whom are outspoken supporters of Palestine—have been severe enough to dissuade other African Americans from debating any subject tied to the country, and this would include conversations with or about white Jews.

As far as I am concerned, Israel consumes the life out of any political discussion about the Middle East. No one wants to put energy into those discussions. At issue is the Jewish community's apparent desire to control African American voices in these debates. This invokes our own trauma and history of subjugation as voiceless subjects.

JB: That's a major and super interesting observation.

TJ: Going back to your point in terms of the Black church, I want to be clear: Progressive traditions do exist within the Black church, but its public face as well as its rhetorical stance remain in far too many instances antiquated and sexist on issues of gender, sexuality, and class. But even within those restrictive settings, Black women in particular have found ways to disrupt the system to support women's leadership and agency.

Your point, however, is focused on Jews and their double consciousness. Of course, we should expect this kind of nuanced perspective from them. However, Blacks don't possess the political or economic power to force Jews to criticize Netanyahu and his horrific settlement policies, while Jews do possess the power to convince elite Blacks to condemn Black antisemitism.

Let's return to your point about white Evangelicals and Jews. Do say more about the allyship between them.

JB: First, let me say forthrightly that the point you just made is important. These Jewish American college kids *do* have a type of political and economic power that is greater than that of their Black counterparts, be they Jewish or not Jewish. I think you've put your finger on an unspoken dilemma. These young Jewish Americans, be they liberal or radical left, don't leverage their power in effective ways when it comes to criticizing Israel. I do not know why that is. It could be a failure of leadership on the left in general. It could be the stranglehold of center-right and right-wing donors on American Jewish discourse. But for whatever reason, many progressive Jewish voices on issues concerning Israel are simply not heard.

The most fascinating discovery in our discussion is the revelation by your colleague, who is pro-Israel and who is tenured yet who still doesn't want to be critical of Israel. In my professional academic societies, believe it or not, I know many Jewish scholars who are afraid to speak at conferences when the parade of anti-Israel critics takes center stage, something it does in academia with astonishing frequency.

TJ: The silencing that happens within the academy is disheartening, and unfortunately, it takes on greater nuance when Blacks and Jews are at the center of the conversation.

One point, however, that I want you to go back to is this idea of allyship. Many American Jews are allied with people who believe in their ultimate destruction vis-à-vis their conversion to Christianity. White Evangelicals appear to be a greater threat to Jews and Israel than a few college kids signing a BDS petition or listening to hyperbolic speeches.

JB: True, but you rarely see friendships developing between white conservative Evangelicals and progressive Jewish students on college campuses. The latter usually don't want to hang out with the former for many reasons, one of which being they don't want to discuss coming to Christ. The friendships that the Jewish kids have with those who aren't Jewish are more likely to be with African American kids.

On the level of "adults," you're absolutely right; that's where the allyship you referred to exists. The Israel lobby's embrace of white conservative Evangelicals is utterly baffling. If you speak to these older Jews, however, they will say it has reaped tremendous rewards for Israel's security and safety.

As for the fraught nature of Black-Jewish dialogue on Israel, take it as a compliment. Jewish Americans care deeply about what African Americans think about them. You know "Molly," although she's a figment of my imagination. She's the Catholic girl from Iowa who wore a keffiyeh and said she hates Israel. When she signs a BDS petition, most Jews on campus aren't surprised or that upset. You know, Molly's gonna Molly. When Black students sign these petitions en masse, for whatever reasons, though, it rankles Jews greatly.

Terrence, I think this goes back to the critique emanating from Black nationalist and Black Power circles that crested in the late 1960s. Jews always noticed how serrated that criticism was, and it surely exposed some vulnerabilities in the tidy Zionist narrative. However, it was a ferocious critique, and I don't know if it opened up possibilities for further dialogue.

TJ: Jacques, does this wrangling stem from the asymmetrical relationships you referenced in chapters 2 and 7? Are Jews upset by these reactions because many African Americans are their caretakers, gardeners, and so forth?

JB: Do you mean to say that Jews aren't used to having African Americans tell them what to do? I think that is part of it. I do believe that has been part of a lot of Black-Jewish dialogue, especially throughout the twentieth century. But what I am speaking about is a form of criticism about Israel advanced by figures such as Stokely Carmichael that was so unrelenting that it didn't permit Jews anywhere to go other than to retreat into particularism and tribalism.

TJ: You seem to be conflating 1960s rhetoric of what SNCC called Third World solidarity and Black internationalism with contemporary debates that imagine Israel as a powerful nation-state. What SNCC initiated in its publication "Third World Round-up: The Palestine Problem: Test Your Knowledge" was a draft of an ongoing discussion in terms of how members should respond to their growing interest in subjugated groups transnationally.[1] Black transnational politics and human rights activism are tied to SNCC's efforts to galvanize African Americans to link anti-Black racism to global struggles against colonialism and class exploitation. Unlike their white Jewish allies, who were increasingly finding room in corporate America and homes in suburbia, SNCC members and their families remained at the bottom of the economic and political well. So I think it's hard to bring in the 1960s debacle because its context is very different from what we're seeing in the current moment.

JB: Actually, Terrence, I think it's the same critique, the same DNA. Such was the acuity of those intellectuals that they created a paradigm for criticizing Israel that is a half-century old and still going strong. It comes up again and again.

You've heard me say a million times in class that Black Power is among the most influential cultural and political movements in American history. So why does it never get its due?

Remember those undergrads on our campus chanting, "From the river to the sea, Palestine must be free"? Jews hear eliminationist overtones in that, just as they did from SNCC's "Third World Round-up" in 1967.

TJ: Jacques, SNCC was not arguing for Israel's elimination. It was arguing for Palestinians and their rights.

JB: That was part of it. Another part of it was casting Israelis as Nazis and calling Israel a white settler colony, erasing the very reason that Jews returned there in the first palace. It erases the existence of Jews of color. It erases the fact that nearly a million Jewish refugees from Arab countries were expelled and had to go somewhere. Many of them went to Israel.

What I'm saying is that the critique was over the top and, as often happened with the Black Power worldview, didn't lead to a way forward that worked within existing discursive structures. Stokely and his crew were visionaries in that regard, but I sometimes worry if

they didn't saddle African Americans with a criticism that was somewhat oblivious to nuances.

TJ: Jacques, as you well know, Black Power activists were also
relentless in their critique of America and "Uncle Toms." What
you were hearing in SNCC's draft proposal is a deep concern with
Israel's denial or seeming refusal to bear witness to its own history
of displacement as it attempted to find refuge for its people.

Part of the reason why Blacks and Jews have had an ongoing and
heated debate on this issue stems from a kind of über set of expectations from each other. They both regard themselves as reflections
and direct descendants of a chosen people, and this shared biblical
mythology seems to cast a cloud over the relationship. I suspect this
also played a critical role in SNCC's criticism of Israel.

As you see, I'm trying to add nuance to the story. What are the
nuances that you think are missing?

JB: For one, Israel and its Arab neighbors jointly, together, made
incredibly idiotic decisions, and one can't easily blame the entire history of warfare and carnage in the region solely on Israel. The second
nuance I would deduce is a categorical misreading of the intention
of Israel's enemies. Their intent *was* to annihilate Israel, and in some
cases it still is, though things are changing in the Arab world.

But what's important, in terms of dialogue, is that when Jews
hear that rhetoric—and that rhetoric continues to this day—they
shut down. Where do Jews go in a free Palestine?

TJ: Again, Jacques, I don't believe SNCC was supportive of the
annihilation of Israel. That being said, Stokely Carmichael and Ethel
Minor, who were considered to be the chief architects of SNCC's
position on Israel, appear to be in favor of good Zionism. What
Carmichael opposed was the Palestinians' displacement as well as
Israel's political relationships with apartheid South Africa.

This brings me back to an earlier point. Carmichael was telling
American Jews that the Zionism that they value did not align with

the Hebrew tradition of social justice and ideologies among the Jewish Left.

JB: Yep, the support for South Africa was deplorable, shortsighted, morally bankrupt, and untenable from an ethical Jewish position.

To your other point, we've both read the scholarship of Clayborne Carson and Keith Feldman about how that fateful SNCC "Third World Round-up" came into being. It seems to have stemmed from a perfect storm of sorts and was likely something that many in SNCC were unaware of. But there it is; it's part of history.

My question for you is this: Jewish critics of Israel, by raising their voices, have had their voices amplified by groups that really do seem bent on the destruction of Israel. What is the proper ethical way forward for principled critics?

TJ: I'm not a historian, nor do I want to rewrite history, but I wonder if SNCC had taken a different political position, what the conversation would look like today. Likewise, what if David Ben-Gurion had found a way to work with anti-colonialists in Africa, or with leftist political movements in Cuba or Central America, or with the Soviet Union? Just a thought.

The Pan-Africanist vision Black Power activists imagined for themselves, as an ethical, political lens, gave way to a vision that reinforced anti-war theories, humanistic strivings, and cultural nationalisms. Of course, this was clearly not the route taken by Israel, but I wonder if the founders had employed a deeply leftist-socialist vision, would it have satisfied not only SNCC but also the critics of Israel.

JB: So then, going back to our students and their positions on Israel, what do you advise those quiet Jewish kids in our class to do when their non-Jewish Black classmates sign BDS petitions?

TJ: They should take the lead from Afro-Christians in regard to the Black church. They should acknowledge Israel's historic and enduring presence for the survival of Jews and Judaism but remain critical of its policies just as many of them condemn America's increasingly visible culture of antisemitism.

Note

1. Student Nonviolent Coordinating Committee (SNCC), "Third World Round-up."

11

Afro-Jews

TJ: Who are Afro-Jews, and how do they complicate scholarly investigations into Blacks and Jews?

JB: That's an ocean of a question. Not being an expert, by any means, I'd still point out there are many different types of Afro-Jews. As you know, in the last couple of decades, scholars such as Lewis Gordon, Edith Bruder, Tudor Parfitt, James Landing, Janice Fernheimer, Nathaniel Deutsch, and Yvonne Chireau have led an explosion of academic interest in Afro-Judaism. Further, with the proliferation of social media, many Afro-Jews are talking about their lives and often tweeting to the white Jewish world (as well as to the racists and antisemites they meet along the way).

Before we go further, I want to ask you, in terms of your professional and personal experiences, what are some of the first things that come to mind when you hear the term "Afro-Jew"?

TJ: I remember the Hebrew Israelite community I stumbled upon in Atlanta, a vibrant group of African Americans that identifies with the African Hebrew Israelites of Jerusalem. The group's two restaurants in Atlanta, called Soul Vegetarian and Soul Vegetarian 2, served as intellectual hubs for artists, activists, and young writers who were looking for healthy food and Black-conscious debates on spirituality, politics, and health when I was a student at Morehouse College in the 1990s. Dressed in stylish African attire and head coverings, the African Hebrew Israelites were highly regarded for their principled, devout, and slightly orthodox theology that valued family, community service, self-help, and entrepreneurship. In fact, they emphasized a vegan diet long before it was popularized by Whole Foods! In many respects, the Soul Vegetarian community offered a counternarrative to the Clinton administration's trope that "Black pathology" was the primary source of poverty in some Black communities.

Before you were a scholar, and just a Jewish Brooklynite who loved and played jazz, whom did you see as Afro-Jews?

JB: My landlord in the 1990s was from Haiti and told me he was Jewish. He lived in the building, and we'd often have backyard parties with all the tenants. We talked about a million subjects, especially racism, but strangely we never talked about Judaism.

When I was younger, a small group of Afro-Jews was a source of endless fascination to white Jews. Want to take a guess who they were, Terrence?

TJ: Were you thinking of Julius Lester, for one?

JB: Bingo! Though I was mostly interested in Lester during my college days. Still, Professor Lester was legendary in Brooklyn through the Ocean Hill–Brownsville episode, so his conversion was a subject of interest.[1]

Who else do you think was in the group?

TJ: Sammy Davis Jr.?

JB: Definitely Sammy Davis Jr. And the baseball player Rod Carew. Remember him? Though, in retrospect, it seems that he was married to a Jewish woman, really admired Judaism, and wore a big old chai necklace, but then it turned out he wasn't actually Jewish. The guy could hit though.

TJ: What about Nell Carter?

JB: Yes! Oh my god, Terrence! You know what this reminds me. The *Saturday Night Live* skit "Jew, Not a Jew" featuring a game show in which contestants competed to figure out who was a member of the tribe and who wasn't. It was weirdly profound, as comedy sometimes is.

Anyhow, I think the watershed moment regarding Afro-Jews was Operation Moses, the airlift of Ethiopian Jews to Israel in 1984. In Israel, a huge public debate raged about Ethiopian Jews as a symbol of how Jews of color (who weren't all necessarily of African descent and included Sephardic and Mizrachi Jews) were treated by the white, Ashkenazi establishment.

Edith Bruder, in *The Black Jews of Africa: History, Religion, and Identity*, teaches us that there's some type of synergy between late nineteenth-century and early twentieth-century African American groups that were Judaizing and a recent surge of African groups that are moving in the same direction, with some converting and some claiming they have been Jews since time immemorial. What is the significance of these Judaizing Black Jewish groups in terms of African American history?

TJ: Black Jewish groups in the United States symbolize in the *flesh* for Blacks in the New World the answer to their perennial search for their origins. Afro-Jews underscore both the rich and nuanced history of African American religions in the Americas, and they point to the "African" presence in the Hebrew Bible and subsequent formation of Judaism. By mapping out the intellectual paths between Israel and Africa, groups such as the African Hebrew Israelites and Harlem's Commandment Keepers found biblical and historical resources to claim a new home for the descendants of African slavery, one where their racialized bodies were transformed through a reencounter with the Hebrew tradition and a metaphoric return to Mount Sinai. The transition to their Hebrew roots was fairly inconsequential, as many of the converts were already familiar with the narratives, symbols, and characters in the Hebrew Bible, most notably the Exodus narrative of Moses leading the children of Israel out of Egypt.

Yvonne Chireau and Nathaniel Deutsch's edited volume *Black Zion* offers a rich historical account of the emergence of Hebrew communities and their pivotal role in shaping Black religion and Black transnational politics. In fact, the volume notes that Rabbi Mordecai Herman, a leading member of Marcus Garvey's Universal Negro Improvement Association, advocated for a shared homeland in Palestine for Afro-Jews and their allies. Many people don't know this history and assume African Americans' interest in Israel and Palestine started during the Black Power movement.

JB: A related point that these scholars make is that some of the descendants of enslaved persons were predisposed to embrace Judaism. The salience of Hebrew Bible themes such as the Exodus story spoke to them. James Landing's book *Black Judaism: Story of an American Movement* was especially helpful in getting me to understand this.

TJ: Embracing Judaism was strangely familiar for many African Americans, especially since many of them would have been introduced to the Hebrew prophets and their social justice commitments through Afro-Christianity. In *A Fire in the Bones: Reflections on African-American Religious History*, Al Raboteau lays out a beautifully written account of how African Americans turned to the prophets in the Old Testament to imagine New World orders during slavery.

Jacques, why are you so interested in the Afro-Jewish element of Judaism?

JB: I think there's a personal reason and an ideological reason for my interest. On the personal level, my mother's side of the family is Sephardic. This means that my whole family in France is from Turkey, Morocco, Algeria, and Tunisia. Were they to walk on American streets, they would not be seen as white (except for the Turks who, strangely, are all fair skinned and blue eyed). I spent my summers in Paris with the Sephardic side, and coming back to Brooklyn, I started to see this subtle racism among white Jews, one that I had imbibed. The older I got the more it perturbed me. So I always felt closely connected to the idea of Jews of color.

In terms of my ideological reason, I have an almost messianic belief that Afro-Jews can bridge crucial divides between white Jewish Americans and non-Jewish African Americans on two crucial issues.

TJ: Your point about the subtle racism you observed is beautifully put and noted. If we look at recent controversies around Black anti-semitism—with DeSean Jackson and Nick Cannon, for instance—what's driving their questions regarding the "true Semitic" people has everything to do with Afro-Jews, the *Blackness* of Judaism.

Edward Blyden, a nineteenth-century Pan-Africanist, writer, and educator, published in 1898 a pamphlet entitled "The Jewish Question." In his short essay, Blyden grappled with the implications of Zionism for African Americans as well as Judaism's roots among the Igbo people in Nigeria.[2] Blyden's work is an example of a long historical link between Blacks and Jews regarding religion, religious identity. On the one hand, his search stemmed from an interest to illuminate a broader history of events in antiquity. On the other hand, African Americans wanted to claim Judaism as theirs.

Jacques, earlier you mentioned two critical issues that Afro-Jews can help bridge. What are they?

JB: Permit me to get to that in one second. I think white Jews in the United States have to have a reckoning in terms of their thinking about their Black coreligionists. Part of the work I do with my synagogue is getting folks there to think really carefully about the complaints that black Jews and Black Jews make about white Jews. What are the complaints? Again and again, they speak of sitting in a synagogue or a Jewish space and getting stares or questions of "why are you here?" and that sort of thing.

So phase 1, and it's probably a long project, is getting organizational American Judaism, which is mostly white, to listen to Jews of African ancestry. It's *so* important that they listen.

I feel that if many types of Afro-Jews are shown the proper respect, and are welcomed and affirmed into white Jewish communities (assuming they want to be there), *then* we can get to those two issues where Afro-Jews can facilitate discussions between gentile

African Americans and white Jews. The first issue is with Jewish white-skin privilege.

TJ: May I interject here? Before you spend time lambasting white Jews for their racist behavior in synagogues, your point belies a deeper issue we ought to face—the demographic of the population inhabiting Judea and what we now call the "Middle East." Put differently, are white Jews willing to embrace Moses, Queen of Shebah, and David as members of an African tribe who were also highly literate in the reigning religious and philosophical traditions of their region?

JB: I would say most Jews would be fine with it, but that's likely because we engage differently with visual and iconic cues. Jews don't have that Norwegian Jesus thing going. You know what I mean? I'm referring to those images of a Scandinavian-looking savior, dressed in a pinkish robe and walking through a meadow with some blond kids skipping alongside him, that abound in white Christendom. The images we Jews see of Moses or Elijah—usually from pre- and early modern Christian painters—really depict swarthy patriarchs and whatnot. So Jews are used to it and probably wouldn't give too much thought to a dark Jacob.

Then again, I'm not a rabbi. I don't get to make enduring Halachic decisions about who is a Jew and who is not a Jew. But quite frankly, I think the time has come in mainstream normative Judaism to departicularize and open up just a bit. Look, if a person wants to be a Jew, let the person be a Jew.

TJ: And in response to your point, Jacques, on the one hand, I think the Jews' history of persecution justifies why they traditionally have been reluctant to welcome and embrace strangers into their synagogues, and I want to respect some of those reasons. On the other hand, I think what I'm referencing is not necessarily the idea of *welcoming* the stranger but is in fact *unearthing* the stranger who is familiar to the tradition.

I'm thinking here of Zora Neale Hurston's novel *Moses, Man of the Mountain*. Hurston reimagines Moses as a conjurer and community healer. In fact, she tells an account of religious history that weaves together Afro-Christianity, indigenous religious practices, and Afro-Jewish interpretations of Moses and his community. To this end, debates on inclusion within contemporary Judaism ignore the deeper historical and theological concerns that African Americans raised after they converted to Judaism.

What was your second suggestion where Afro-Jews could help bridge the divide between white Jewish Americans and non-Jewish African Americans?

JB: Israel/Palestine. So much of the criticism of Israel—from the Suez Canal Crisis, to the Black Power movement, to Israel's ill-advised diplomatic relations with South Africa—has been that Israel is a white colonial outpost in a much darker Middle Eastern and African neighborhood. The truth of the matter is, Terrence, that more than half of Israel's Jewish population is people of color. That's the first thing that Americans who have never been there notice when they visit. To wit, the country is dark. And that's because Judaism is dark.

By having Afro-Jews—and I mean Afro-Jews who have been given the right to emigrate to Israel and become citizens of the Jewish state—speak to non-Jewish persons of African ancestry about the word- and thought-defying complexity of the Israeli-Palestinian conflict, I feel, could create possibilities for dialogue on all sides. And it might be a way to bring Palestinian interlocutors aboard as well.

TJ: I, too, recall my first experience in Israel, and I agree with your assessment. Whether I was in Tel Aviv or Jerusalem, I was overwhelmed by the presence of non-white Jews in the Holy Land. Unfortunately, the picturesque scenes belied the increasing concerns of racism, at least during the 1990s, experienced by Ethiopian Jews, from the lack of a Black presence within the Israeli government, and from the dehumanization of Palestinians.

JB: Absolutely. They are maddening issues in Israel for folks of African ancestry, be they from the Maghreb or the Horn. I don't want to sound like an apologist, but I do think and hope that the situation is improving. I know that we Sephardic Jews complained about our treatment for decades, and then gradually things did get better in Israel. I'm also encouraged that the Hebrew Israelites, whom you mentioned earlier, seem to have found a home in Israel in Dimona. All of that makes me guardedly optimistic.

Naturally, the fact that we're even having this discussion suggests that Judaism needs a real reckoning about race. And that's why I think the future of Blacks and Jews dialogue should be routed through Afro-Jews.

On a personal note, in my family we always talk about voting with our feet and leaving our overwhelmingly white synagogue—which we really like and which has always been wonderful to us, but the rabbi is cool and would understand this—and joining an Afro-Jewish synagogue, assuming it would take us. Big if, that. A problem is that a lot of those synagogues are not liberal on social issues, and we are. But I'd hope we could find one, and if the people would accept us, and tens of thousands more like us, I think more dialogue and trust would be created.

TJ: Your idealism here is unusual and unexpected. You are generally far more critical of those who embrace pluralism and actually believe it is possible today.

But more important, we are missing a bigger point. In my experience with the Hebrew Israelites of Atlanta, many of them seemed to reject racially constructed categories that reinforced the white normative gaze. Instead, they defined themselves unequivocally as Hebrews. In your pursuit of a culturally rich Afro-Jewish synagogue, you will likely find people who decry racial categories and instead imagine themselves as post-Black. I can't wait to read about your observations when you find and join this community!

JB: Yes, you totally get what I'm thinking. One last thing: Again, I was really touched by that Lewis Gordon essay where he asked why Jews who celebrate Passover always talk about slavery in Egypt but forgo discussions of slavery in the United States.[3] It reminds me that the best Passover I have ever had was when we invited some friends over who were gentile African Americans. Ten people were at the seder, and everyone "got" it.

TJ: Lewis's point hits hard and exposes the limits of rituals that are retrieved to affirm and legitimate a sealed past. He's not only exposing the parochial nature of rituals but also pushing white Jews to come to terms with the enduring legacy of their racialized past and their indelible ancestral connection through the enslavement of African Americans. The recognition of such a clear bond between them would lead inevitably to the radicalization of Judaism, one in which, as you hope, will place Afro-Jews at the center of Judaism.

Notes

1. Harris, *Ocean Hill–Brownsville Conflict*.
2. Blyden, "Jewish Question."
3. Gordon, "Afro-Jewish Ethics?," in Hutt, Kim, and Lerner, *Jewish Religious and Philosophical Ethics*, 213–27.

12

Outro

JB: Terrence, we somehow managed to finish this book. Our families will be relieved! Before we talk about each other's work, let's take a run at this question: In the research you did for *Blacks and Jews in America: An Invitation to Dialogue*, what surprised you the most, upended a truth you took for granted, made you reassess a cherished assumption?

TJ: I took for granted the long and winding history of Afro-Jews in the United States. Of course, we read each year Lewis Gordon's "Rarely Kosher: Studying Jews of Color in North America," but as I dived into Yvonne Chireau and Nathaniel Deutsch's *Black Zion*, I realized how much I had vastly underestimated the depth and rich religious anthropology within African American religions.

Dating back to the late eighteenth century, African Americans encountered and embraced Judaism in a myriad of contexts with sometimes-competing theological interests. Some of them, such as the Kansas-based Church of God and Saints of Christ, blended Christian and Jewish traditions within their worship and theological views; others, such as the Hebrew Israelites, believed the children of Israel were Black. Some, such as Chicago's Rabbi Capers Funnye Jr., were raised Christian (African Methodist Episcopal) but converted to Judaism after growing dissatisfied with Christianity. (In fact, Funnye has converted twice!)

What I find fascinating is the fluidity of religious life among a people who are often mischaracterized as conservative or rigid when it comes to religion. What this also demonstrates is the potential for religious sources to speak in and beyond their textual boundaries. Among many of the African American converts to Judaism in the twentieth century, Rabbi Alysa Stanton, for example, traces her conversion to her time spent with her Christian grandmother. If I recall correctly, Rabbi Stanton said in an interview that one day when her grandmother read from the Old Testament, Stanton knew God or the characters were talking directly to her. She knew then that she was being moved religiously and spiritually in a new direction.

The hermeneutical and spiritual engagement with religious texts among these African Americans is extraordinary. It speaks to their creative geniuses.

What about you, Jacques? What did you rethink while writing this book?

JB: For me, I reconsidered southern Jewry. My readings on Jews of the South made me realize we don't do enough about this in our class. Further, the scholarship is unsettled on the question of the interrelationship between Jewish whiteness and the South. Karen Brodkin in *How Jews Became White Folks* presents Jews as being racially reassigned to whiteness in the aftermath of World War II, but the scholarship I read suggests that in the antebellum period, Jews in the South had *already* achieved this status. I mean, you don't get to be secretary of state of the Confederacy, as Judah Benjamin did, if your group's white status is dubious!

The arrival in the South of eastern European Jews after 1881 (as opposed to the German and Sephardic ones who were there prior to 1848, at which point central European Jews trickled in) complexifies matters. The eastern Europeans were clearly of a different type, and as the studies show, they had far fewer racial hang-ups. I don't know how "white" those eastern European southern Jews were considered to be in the early twentieth century, and I certainly don't think they wanted to be white.

One last thing: the southern example also teaches us that Jewish whiteness can be revoked. Whenever Jews supported desegregation and civil rights legislation, or advocated for communist causes, their standing as white was rendered wobbly. The Jews of the South understood this, likely through the expedient of having their synagogues bombed and stores burned by the local white supremacists. This accounts for the southern Jews' cautious (some might say cowardly) postures on civil rights and why they behaved so differently from northern Jews during the 1940s through the 1960s.

> **TJ:** You have commented a lot on Israel and Black Power. Can you say more about the kind of subnarratives that surround these issues, things that don't make the headlines?

JB: Having worked a lot on fiction, I can only say that a host of compelling narratives lay behind the Black Power movement as it pertains to Blacks and Jews. Black Power emerged in the 1960s, but actual, real face-to-face relationships between Blacks and Jews were commonplace in the North from the 1920s onward. Blacks and Jews were not strangers to one another in 1967 when SNCC shunted whites out of the organization. They had decades of intense encounters behind them. That's what I think we mean by "subnarratives."

We both find it intriguing that a figure such as Stokely Carmichael had a deep connection with Jews in his younger days. (Another similar figure is Professor Leonard Jeffries.) Then there were all those women Debra Schultz studied in *Going South: Jewish Women in the Civil Rights Movement*. Again, the relationships were so close, so intimate between the Jewish American and non-Jewish African American activists.

In one of our discussions, we lamented the absence of real relationships nowadays between Blacks and Jews. Say what you will about the 1960s, until the purges (and even afterward), there were lots of interactions, for better or for worse.

> **TJ:** Let's move from structures to individuals. Who do you find yourself thinking about now that the research is done?

JB: The person I think about often is Andrew Young. I feel he was a great man who got caught in the maws of the Israeli-Palestinian conflict *and* the Blacks and Jews conflict *and* the fecklessness of Jimmy Carter's foreign policy shop. He clearly deserved better.

What about you? Who is an individual you're thinking about now at the end of this particular project?

TJ: I feel intimately connected to Rabbi Abraham Heschel's spirit. There's something deeply profound in his relationship to the Black struggle. He opened himself to the Negro spirituals, and he listened to their message. This might explain why he believed humankind's future could be found, possibly, in African American spirituals.

Many people listen to the music, but do many "hear" the ancestors in it? Rabbi Heschel heard them.

JB: My next question for you concerns liberalism, your topic in chapter 3. I understand the concerns you expressed, but what replaces liberalism?

TJ: Great question! I don't know the answer, but more important, I don't want to come up with its replacement. The struggle against the tradition is more important than finding a specific response to it. What I'm discovering as I become more intimate with Africana philosophy and Black radical traditions is that I am increasingly less interested in engaging liberalism on its terms. And maybe one day I won't talk about it at all.

Regarding your work in chapter 2, what do you want white Jews to walk away with after they've read your critical assessment of the history of racism in Jewish communities?

JB: I want them to listen—to listen to the African American folks and to listen to what so many scholars and rabbis and activists in the community have been saying. Listen to the things you don't like to hear!

TJ: From March 2020 to September 2020, as we wrote this book, we witnessed a lot. What's your takeaway in terms of the next steps for what you call "*Blacks and Jews"?

JB: What haven't we seen in the last few months? Agreeing to disagree about Israel/Palestine is what I feel is the next hurdle for white Jewish and Black Lives Matter activists. If they can somehow find a way to do that, then I would not discount the power of that alliance.

In my studies of American secularism, I have noticed that whenever evangelical Christians and the American Roman Catholic Church, via its bishops, teamed up on an issue (which is easier said than done, given their history), they were like a juggernaut, a formidable political force. Think about the headway those groups have made on abortion, school vouchers, and every manner of ordinance against LGBTQ people.

Although much smaller, the union of *Blacks and Jews in this moment has the potential to be very effective. The idea of affinity groups is where I would invest my stock. Yet those conversations have to be hosted and organized, and the groundwork must be done by institutions with resources to commit to this effort. And it can't be conducted on an unequal playing field. I'd like to see some deep-pocketed donors, both African American and Jewish American, invest in this effort. There should be dialogue, but more important, it should include projects, actual goal-oriented projects.

What's your takeaway in terms of the next steps on *Blacks and Jews?

TJ: We're a beautiful people—wounded, in exile, and broken. Beautiful. My takeaway from this moment is to tell the truth. Then to turn truth into action.

I can't stomach another conversation on Minister Farrakhan's dislike of the Jews or on Jewish American wealth as evidence of the Jews' complicity in white supremacy. Those arguments are creative excuses to justify the status quo, to keep us firmly tucked away within our respective tribes.

This year has been a year of death meted by evil people and institutions. *They* will continue to try to kill us.

I want to find *life* in this horrible moment, to find life in the struggle, to find life in our beauty. Both groups need to turn inward before imagining any partnerships or conversations with each other.

Truth telling within our respective communities—behind closed doors—is fundamental and necessary.

The "Jew"—real and perceived—must be confronted. When and if Blacks decide to share their pain with their Jewish brothers and sisters, the latter must be open to hearing them. African Americans should also remain open to hearing Jews express the pain and frustration they feel from Black and Jewish encounters.

The life we yearn to embody depends on Blacks and Jews both reckoning with our intertwined histories, as painful as it may be.

ACKNOWLEDGMENTS

We thank the students who enrolled in our Blacks and Jews in America course over the past several years at Georgetown University. They provided invaluable insight into the concerns facing emerging leaders within Black and Jewish communities. We are indebted to our student researchers, Alexander Lin and Ria Pradhan, for spending an entire summer in the midst of a worldwide pandemic to help us complete the work.

Both of us extend our appreciation to Georgetown University's Lauinger Library and Mr. Jeffrey Popovich who was very kind in helping us procure materials during the COVID lockdown.

We wish to thank the Georgetown University Press for supporting our project, and we especially acknowledge the production and marketing staffs.

Last, we thank our agent Michael Mungiello of InkWell agency for believing in this project and helping to bring it to fruition.

INTERVIEWEES

Yvonne Chireau is a professor in the Department of Religion at Swarthmore College, where she teaches courses on African American religions, American religious history, and folk and popular religions. She is the author of *Black Magic: Religion and the African American Conjuring Tradition* (University of California Press), the coeditor of *Black Zion: African American Religions and Judaism* (Oxford University Press), and the creator of the website Academic Hoodoo.

Susannah Heschel is the Eli M. Black Distinguished Professor and chair of the Jewish Studies Program at Dartmouth College. Her scholarship focuses on the history of Jewish and Protestant religious thought in Germany during the nineteenth and twentieth centuries. She is the author of *Abraham Geiger and the Jewish Jesus* (University of Chicago Press) and *The Aryan Jesus: Christian Theologians and the Bible in Nazi Germany* (Princeton University Press). She has also edited several volumes, including *Insider/Outsider: American Jews and Multiculturalism* (University of California Press) and *Betrayal: German Churches and the Holocaust* (Fortress Press). She is the author of over a hundred articles and has edited two volumes of her father's writings, including *Moral Grandeur and Spiritual Audacity: Writings of Abraham Joshua Heschel* (Farrar, Straus and Giroux). Her current research focuses on the history of European Jewish scholarship on Islam, and she published her first book on that topic, in German, *Jüdischer Islam: Islam und jüdisch-deutsche Selbstbestimmung* (Matthes & Seitz). She has also published a coedited volume with Umar Ryad, *The Muslim Reception of European Orientalism* (Routledge).

BIBLIOGRAPHY

Adams, Maurianne, and John Bracey, eds. *Strangers and Neighbors: Relations between Blacks and Jews in the United States.* Amherst: University of Massachusetts Press, 1999.

Adderly, Cannonball. *Cannonball Adderley's Fiddler on the Roof.* Scranton: Capitol Records, T 2216, 1964. Compact disc.

African American Policy Forum. "Kimberlé Crenshaw on Intersectionality, More than Two Decades Later." African American Policy Forum, Columbia Law School, June 8, 2017. https://www.law.columbia.edu/news/archive/kimberle-crenshaw-intersectionality-more-two-decades-later.

Anderson, Carol. *Bourgeois Radicals: The NAACP and the Struggle for Colonial Liberation, 1941–1960.* New York: Cambridge University Press, 2015.

Anti-Defamation League. *Malcolm X on the Record: An Analysis of His Views on Race, Jews and Israel, on Civil Rights.* New York: Anti-Defamation League, 1992.

Azoulay, Katya Gibel. *Black, Jewish, and Interracial: It's Not the Color of Your Skin, but the Race of Your Kin, and Other Myths of Identity.* Durham NC: Duke University Press, 1997.

Baker, Ella, and Marvel Cooke. "The Bronx Slave Market (1935)." In Adams and Bracey, *Strangers and Neighbors,* 369–74.

Baldwin, James. "Negroes Are Anti-Semitic because They're Anti-White." In Berman, *Blacks and Jews,* 31–41.

BBC News. "Charleston Church Shooting: Nine Die in South Carolina 'Hate Crime.'" June 18, 2015. https://www.bbc.com/news/world-us-canada-33179019.

Beatty, Paul. *Tuff.* New York: Anchor, 2001.

Beck, Evelyn Torton. "The Politics of Jewish Invisibility." *National Women's Studies Association Journal* 1 (1988): 93–102.

Bellow, Saul. *Mr. Sammler's Planet.* New York: Viking, 1970.

Bender, Eugene. "Reflections on Negro-Jewish Relationships: The Historical Dimension." *Phylon* 30 (1969): 56–65.

Ben-Jochannan, Yosef. *We the Black Jews: Witness to the "White Jewish Race" Myth.* New York: Alkebu-lan Books and Education Materials Associates, 1983.

Benor, Sarah Bunin. "Black and Jewish: Language and Multiple Strategies for Self-Presentation." *American Jewish History* 100 (January 2016): 51–71.

Berkovits, Balázs. "Critical Whiteness Studies and the 'Jewish Problem.'" *Zeitschrift für kritische Sozialtheorie und Philosophie* 5 (2018): 86–102.

Berlinerblau, Jacques. *Campus Confidential: How College Works, or Doesn't, for Professors, Parents, and Students.* New York: Melville House, 2017.

———. *Heresy in the University: The Black Athena Controversy and the Responsibilities of American Intellectuals.* New Brunswick NJ: Rutgers University Press, 1999.

———. *How to Be Secular: A Call to Arms for Religious Freedom.* Boston: Houghton Mifflin Harcourt, 2012.

Berman, Lila Corwin. "American Jews and the Ambivalence of Middle-Classness." *American Jewish History* 93, no. 4 (2007): 409–34.

Berman, Paul, ed. *Blacks and Jews: Alliances and Arguments.* New York: Delacorte, 1994.

Berson, Lenora. *The Negroes and the Jews.* New York: Random House, 1971.

Blyden, Edward Wilmot. "The Jewish Question." Liverpool: Lionel Hart, 1898.

Bond, Julian. Introduction. In Adams and Bracey, *Strangers and Neighbors,* 1–16.

Bowman, Emma, Gabriela Saldivia, and Shannon Van Sant. "Suspect Charged with 29 Federal Counts in Pittsburgh Synagogue Massacre." *NPR,* October 27, 2018. https://www.npr.org/2018/10/27/661347236/multiple-casualties-in-shooting-near-pittsburgh-synagogue.

Brodkin, Karen. *How Jews Became White Folks and What That Says about Race in America.* New Brunswick NJ: Rutgers University Press, 1994.

Brotz, Howard. *The Black Jews of Harlem: Negro Nationalism and the Dilemmas of Negro Leadership.* New York: Free Press of Glencoe, 1964.

———. "Negro 'Jews' in the United States." *Phylon* 13 (1952): 324–37.

Bruder, Edith. *The Black Jews of Africa: History, Religion, Identity.* Oxford: Oxford University Press, 2008.

Bruder, Edith, and Tudor Parfitt, eds. *African Zion: Studies in Black Judaism.* Newcastle: Cambridge Scholars' Publishing, 2012.

Buddick, Emily. *Blacks and Jews in Literary Conversation.* New York: Cambridge University Press, 1998.

Buhle, Paul, and Robin Kelley. "Allies of a Different Sort: Jews and Blacks in the American Left." In Salzman and West, *Struggles in the Promised Land*, 197–229.

Callahan, Allen Dwight. *The Talking Book: African Americans and the Bible*. New Haven CT: Yale University Press, 2006.

Carbin, Maria, and Sara Edenheim. "The Intersectional Turn in Feminist Theory: A Dream of a Common Language?" *European Journal of Women's Studies* 20 (2013): 233–48. https://journals.sagepub.com/doi/10.1177/13505 06813484723.

Carmichael, Stokely. *Stokely Speaks: From Black Power to Pan-Africanism*. Chicago: Chicago Review Press, 2007.

Carson, Clayborne. "Blacks and Jews in the Civil Rights Movement." In Adams and Bracey, *Strangers and Neighbors*, 574–89.

———. *In Struggle: SNCC and the Black Awakening of the 1960s*. Cambridge MA: Harvard University Press, 1995.

———. "The Politics of Relations between African-Americans and Jews." In Berman, *Blacks and Jews*, 131–43.

Chanes, Jerome. "Affirmative Action, Jewish Ideals, Jewish Interests." In Salzman and West, *Struggles in the Promised Land*, 295–321.

Chazan, Naomi. "The Fallacies of Pragmatism: Israeli Foreign Policy toward South Africa." In Washington, *Jews in Black Perspectives*, 148–81.

Chireau, Yvonne. *Black Magic: Religion and the African American Conjuring Tradition*. Berkeley: University of California Press, 2003.

Chireau, Yvonne, and Nathaniel Deutsch, eds. *Black Zion: African American Religious Encounters with Judaism*. New York: Oxford University Press, 2000.

———. Introduction. In Chireau and Deutsch, *Black Zion*, 3–11.

Cobb, Jelani. "The Matter of Black Lives." *New Yorker*, March 14, 2016. https://www.newyorker.com/magazine/2016/03/14/where-is-black-lives-matter-headed.

Collins, Patricia Hill. "Intersectionality's Definitional Dilemmas." *Annual Review of Sociology* 41 (2015): 1–20.

Crenshaw, Kimberlé. "Demarginalizing the Intersection of Race and Sex: A Black Feminist Critique of Antidiscrimination Doctrine, Feminist Theory and Antiracist Politics." *University of Chicago Legal Forum* 1 (1989): 139–67. http://chicagounbound.uchicago.edu/uclf/vol1989/iss1/8.

Cruse, Harold. *The Crisis of the Negro Intellectual*. New York: William Morrow, 1967.

———. "My Jewish Problem and Theirs." In Hentoff, *Black Anti-Semitism*, 143–90.

Davis, David Brion. "Jews in the Slave Trade." In Salzman and West, *Struggles in the Promised Land*, 65–72.

Diner, Hasia. "Between Words and Deeds." In Salzman and West, *Struggles in the Promised Land*, 87–106.

———. "Drawn Together by Self-Interest: Jewish Representations of Race and Race Relations in the Early Twentieth Century." In Franklin et al., *African Americans and Jews*, 27–39.

———. *In the Almost Promised Land: American Jews and Blacks, 1915–1933*. Westport CT: Greenwood Press, 1977.

———. *Julius Rosenwald: Repairing the World*. New Haven CT: Yale University Press, 2017.

Dollinger, Marc. *Black Power, Jewish Politics: Reinventing the Alliance in the 1960s*. Waltham MA: Brandeis University Press, 2018.

———. "'Hamans' and 'Torquemadas': Southern and Northern Jewish Responses to the Civil Rights Movement, 1945–1965." In *The Quiet Voices: Southern Rabbis and Black Civil Rights, 1880s to 1990s*, edited by Mark Bauman and Berkley Kalin, 67–94. Tuscaloosa: University of Alabama Press, 1997.

———. *Quest for Inclusion: Jews and Liberalism in Modern America*. Princeton NJ: Princeton University Press, 2000.

Dorman, Jacob. *Chosen People: The Rise of American Black Israelite Religions*. Oxford: Oxford University Press, 2013.

———. "'I Saw You Disappear with My Own Eyes': Hidden Transcripts of New York Black Israelite Bricolage." *Nova Religio* 11 (2007): 61–83.

Drescher, Seymour. "Jews and New Christians in the Atlantic Slave Trade." In Sarna and Mendelsohn, *Jews and the Civil War*, 51–86.

———. "The Role of Jews in the Transatlantic Slave Trade." In Adams and Bracey, *Strangers and Neighbors*, 105–16.

Du Bois, W. E. B. (William Edward Burghardt). "As the crow flies, December 7, 1940." W. E. B. Du Bois Papers (MS 312). Special Collections and University Archives, University of Massachusetts, Amherst Libraries.

———. "Of Our Spiritual Strivings." *The Souls of Black Folk*. Mineola NY: Dover Publications, 1994.

Evans, Eli. *The Provincials: A Personal History of Jews in the South*. New York: Free Press, 1997.

Fanon, Frantz. *The Wretched of the Earth*. New York: Grove Press, 2004.

Feldman, Keith P. *A Shadow over Palestine: The Imperial Life of Race in America*. Minneapolis: University of Minnesota Press, 2015.

Fernheimer, Janice. *Stepping into Zion: Hatzaad Harishon, Black Jews, and the Remaking of Jewish Identity*. Tuscaloosa: University of Alabama Press, 2014.

Flores, Nicole. *The Aesthetics of Solidarity: Our Lady of Guadalupe and American Democracy*. Washington DC: Georgetown University Press, 2021.

Forman, Seth. *Blacks in the Jewish Mind: A Crisis of Liberalism*. New York: New York University Press, 1998.

———. "The Unbearable Whiteness of Being Jewish: Desegregation in the South and the Crisis of Jewish Liberalism." *American Jewish History* 85 (1997): 121–42.

Forward. "Rachel Gilmer: The Jewish Heart of #BlackLivesMatter." https://forward.com/series/forward-50/2016/rachel-gilmer/.

Franklin, V. P. "The Portrayal of Jews in *The Autobiography of Malcolm X*." In Franklin et al., *African Americans and Jews*, 293–308.

Franklin, V. P., Nancy L. Grant, Harold M. Kletnick, and Genna Rae McNeil, eds. *African Americans and Jews in the Twentieth Century: Studies in Convergence and Conflict*. Columbia: University of Missouri Press, 1998.

Friedman, Murray. "Intergroup Relations." *American Jewish Year Book* 81 (1981): 121–33.

———. *What Went Wrong? The Creation and Collapse of the Black-Jewish Alliance*. New York: Free Press, 1994.

Friedman, Saul. *Jews and the American Slave Trade*. New Brunswick NJ: Transaction, 2000.

Gardiner, Charles, et al. "The Future of the Negro." *The North American Review* 139 (July 1884). https://www.jstor.org/stable/pdf/25118403.pdf.

Garza, Alicia. "Asking My Jewish Friends: The Anti-Semitism and the Anti-Black Racism of the Right Is Exhausting." Facebook, August 19, 2017. https://www.facebook.com/ChasingGarza/posts/d41d8cd9/1978494602422205/.

Gilbert, Kenyatta R. *Pursued Justice: Black Preaching from the Great Migration to Civil Rights*. Waco TX: Baylor University Press, 2016.

Gilkes, Cheryl Townsend. "'Go and Tell Mary and Martha': The Spirituals, Biblical Options for Women, and Cultural Tensions in the African American Religious Experience." *Social Compass* 43, no. 4 (1996): 563–81.

Giroux, Henry A. "Donald Trump and Neo-Fascism in America." *Arena Magazine* 140 (2016): 31–32.

Glaude, Eddie, Jr. *Exodus! Religion, Race, and Nation in Early Nineteenth-Century Black America*. Chicago: University of Chicago Press, 2000.

Glazer, Nathan. "Jews and Blacks: What Happened to the Grand Alliance?" In Washington, *Jews in Black Perspectives*, 105–12.

Goetschel, Willi. "Spinoza's Dream." *Cambridge Journal of Postcolonial Literary Inquiry* 3, no. 1 (2016): 39.

Goffman, Ethan. *Imagining Each Other: Blacks and Jews in Contemporary American Literature.* Albany: State University of New York Press, 2000.

Gold, Roberta. "The Black Jews of Harlem: Representation, Identity, and Race, 1920–1939." *American Quarterly* 55 (2003): 179–225.

Goldberg, J. J. *Jewish Power: Inside the American Jewish Establishment.* New York: Basic Books, 1996.

Goldstein, Eric L. *The Price of Whiteness: Jews, Race, and Identity.* Princeton NJ: Princeton University Press, 2006.

Gooding-Williams, Robert. "Politics, Racial Solidarity, Exodus!" *Journal of Speculative Philosophy* 18, no. 2 (2004): 118–28.

Gordon, Jane Anna. "What Should Blacks Think When Jews Choose Whiteness? An Ode to Baldwin." *Critical Philosophy of Race* 3 (2015): 227–58.

Gordon, Lewis R. "Afro-Jewish Ethics?" In *Jewish Religious and Philosophical Ethics*, edited by Curtis Hutt, Halla Kim, and Berel Lerner, 213–27. London: Routledge, 2018.

——. *Bad Faith and Antiblack Racism.* Atlantic Highlands NJ: Humanities Press, 1995.

——. "Race, Theodicy, and the Normative Emancipatory Challenges of Blackness." *South Atlantic Quarterly* 112, no. 4 (Fall 2013): 725–36.

——. "Rarely Kosher: Studying Jews of Color in North America." *American Jewish History* 100 (2016): 105–16.

——. "Réflexions sur la question afro-juive." *Plurielles: Revue culturelle et politique pour un judaïsme humaniste et Laïque* 16 (2011): 75–82.

——. "Review of Falguni A. Sheth: *Toward a Political Philosophy of Race.*" *Continental Philosophy Review* 44 (2011): 119–30.

——. *What Fanon Said: A Philosophical Introduction to His Life and Thought.* New York: Fordham University Press, 2015.

Gordon, Lewis, and Linda Alcoff. "A Philosophical Account of Africana Studies: An Interview with Lewis Gordon." *Nepantla: Views from South* 4 (2003): 165–89.

Gordon, Lewis, and Sonia Dayan-Herzbrun. "Pourquoi les juifs ne doivent pas redouter la libération." *Tumultes* 1 (2018): 97–108.

Greenberg, Cheryl Lynn. "'I'm Not White—I'm Jewish': The Racial Politics of American Jews." In Sicher, *Race, Color, Identity*, 35–55.

——. *Troubling the Waters: Black-Jewish Relations in the American Century.* Princeton NJ: Princeton University Press, 2006.

Greenberg, Mark. "Becoming Southern: The Jews of Savannah, Georgia, 1830–70." *American Jewish History* 86 (1998): 55–75.

Greenebaum, Jessica. "Placing Jewish Women into the Intersectionality of Race, Class and Gender." *Race, Gender & Class* 6 (1999): 41–60.

Gurock, Jeffrey. *The Jews of Harlem: The Rise, Decline, and Revival of a Jewish Community.* New York: New York University Press, 2016.

Gutman, Herbert. "Parallels in the Urban Experience." In Washington, *Jews in Black Perspectives*, 98–104.

Harris, Glen Anthony. *The Ocean Hill–Brownsville Conflict: Intellectual Struggles between Blacks and Jews at Mid-Century.* Lanham MD: Lexington Books, 2012.

Harrison-Kahan, Lori. "Scholars and Knights: W.E.B. Du Bois, J. E. Spingarn, and the NAACP." *Jewish Social Studies* 18 (2011): 63–87.

Hart, William D. *Edward Said and the Religious Effects of Culture.* Cambridge: Cambridge University Press, 2000.

Haynes, Bruce. "A Member of the Club? How Black Jews Negotiate Black Anti-Semitism and Jewish Racism." In Sicher, *Race, Color, Identity*, 147–66.

———. "People of God, Children of Ham: Making Black(s) Jews." *Journal of Modern Jewish Studies* 8 (2009): 237–54.

———. *The Soul of Judaism: Jews of African Descent in America.* New York: New York University Press, 2018.

Hellwig, David. "Black Images of Jews: From Reconstruction to Depression." In Adams and Bracey, *Strangers and Neighbors*, 300–315.

Hentoff, Nat, ed. *Black Anti-Semitism and Jewish Racism.* New York: Schocken Books, 1972.

Herrnstein, Richard, and Charles Murray. *The Bell Curve: Intelligence and Class Structure in American Life.* New York: Free Press, 1994.

Heschel, Abraham Joshua. "Religion and Race (1963)." *BlackPast*, August 12, 2017. https://www.blackpast.org/african-american-history/1963-rabbi-abraham -joshua-heschel-religion-and-race/.

Heschel, Abraham, and Susannah Heschel. *Abraham Joshua Heschel: Essential Writings.* Maryknoll NY: Orbis Books, 2011.

Higginbotham, Evelyn Brooks. "African American Women's History and the Metalanguage of Race." *Signs* 17, no. 2 (1992): 251–74.

Hill, Robert. "Black Zionism: Marcus Garvey and the Jewish Question." In Franklin et al., *African Americans and Jews*, 40–53.

Himes, Chester. *Lonely Crusade.* New York: De Capo, 1997.

Himmelfarb, Milton. "Negroes, Jews, and Muzhiks." In Rose, *Ghetto and Beyond*, 409–18.

Holden, Matthew, Jr. "Reflections on Two Isolated Peoples." In Washington, *Jews in Black Perspectives*, 182–211.

hooks, bell. "Keeping a Legacy of Shared Struggle." In Berman, *Blacks and Jews*, 229–38.

Hurston, Zora Neale. *Moses, Man of the Mountain.* Philadelphia: J. B. Lippincott, 1939.

Isaacs, Anna. "Feeling Torn over Black Lives Platform, Young Jews Discuss the Way Forward." *Moment Magazine*, August 16, 2016. https://moment mag.com/feeling-torn-black-lives-platform-young-jews-discuss-way -forward/.

———. "How the Black Lives Matter and Palestinian Movements Converged." *Moment Magazine*, March 14, 2016. https://momentmag.com/22800-2/?_ga =2.239111235.1923467096.1595684986-544543450.1595684986.

Jabaily, Annalisa. "1967: How Estrangement and Alliances between Blacks, Jews, and Arabs Shaped a Generation of Civil Rights Family Values." *Law & Inequality* 23 (2005): 197–237.

Jackson, John, Jr. *Thin Description: Ethnography and the African Hebrew Israelites of Jerusalem.* Cambridge MA: Harvard University Press, 2013.

Jacobson, Matthew Frye. *Barbarian Virtues: The United States Encounters Foreign Peoples at Home and Abroad, 1876–1917.* New York: Hill and Wang, 2000.

James, Joy. "Ella Baker, 'Black Women's Work' and Activist Intellectuals." *The Black Scholar* 24, no. 4 (2015): 8–15.

Johnson, Terrence. Interview by Jericka Duncan. "Holocaust Survivor Says NFL Star DeSean Jackson Accepted Invitation to Auschwitz after Anti-Semitic Post." CBS News, July 22, 2020. https://www.cbsnews.com/news /desean-jackson-anti-semitic-post-holocaust-survivor-auschwitz/.

———. "On the Limits of Rights and Reason: The Moral Challenge of Blackness and the Problem of Public Reason." *Journal of Religious Ethics* 43, no. 4 (2014): 697–722.

Jonas, Gilbert. *Freedom's Sword: The NAACP and the Struggle against Racism in America, 1909–1969.* New York: Routledge, 2005.

Jones, Bartlett. *Flawed Triumphs: Andy Young at the United Nations.* Lanham MD: University Press of America, 1996.

Kaplan, Benjamin. "Judah Philip Benjamin." In *Jews in the South,* edited by Leonard Dinnerstein and Mary Palsson, 75–88. Baton Rouge: Louisiana State University Press, 1973.

Katz, Mickey. *Don Byron Plays the Music of Mickey Katz.* With Don Byron, conducted by Don Byron. New York: Nonesuch 7559-79313, 1993. Compact disc.

Kaufman, Jonathan. "Blacks and Jews: The Struggles in the Cities." In Salzman and West, *Struggles in the Promised Land*, 107–21.

Kaufmann, Jay. "Thou Shalt Surely Rebuke Thy Neighbor." In Hentoff, *Black Anti-Semitism and Jewish Racism*, 43–76.

Kaye/Kantrowitz, Melanie. *The Colors of Jews: Racial Politics and Radical Diasporism*. Bloomington: Indiana University Press, 2007.

Kelley, Robin D. G. *Hammer and Hoe: Alabama Communists during the Great Depression*. 25th anniversary ed. Chapel Hill: University of North Carolina Press, 2015.

Kelman, Ari Y., Aaron Hahn Tapper, Izabel Fonseca, and Aliya Saperstein. "Counting the Inconsistencies: An Analysis of American Jewish Population Studies with a Focus on Jews of Color." Jews of Color Field Building Initiative, 2019. https://jewsofcolorfieldbuilding.org/wp-content/uploads/2019/05/Counting-Inconsistencies-052119.pdf.

Kenan, Randall. "The Good Ship Jesus: Baldwin, Bergman, and the Protestant Imagination; or, Baldwin's Bitter Taste." *African American Review* 46, no. 4 (2013): 712–71.

Klapper, Melissa. *Ballots, Babies, and Banners of Peace: American Jewish Women's Activism, 1890–1940*. New York: New York University Press, 2013.

Korn, Bertram. "Jews and Negro Slavery in the Old South, 1789–1865." In *Jews in the South*, edited by Leonard Dinnerstein and Mary Palsson, 89–134. Baton Rouge: Louisiana State University Press, 1973.

Lackey, Michael. "Moses, Man of Oppression: A Twentieth-Century African American Critique of Western Theocracy." *African American Review* 43, no. 4 (2009): 582–83.

Landes, Ruth. "Negro Jews in Harlem." *Jewish Journal of Sociology* 9 (1967): 175–90.

Landing, James. *Black Judaism: Story of an American Movement*. Durham NC: Carolina Academic Press, 2002.

Lee, Jennifer. *Civility in the City: Blacks, Jews, and Koreans in Urban America*. Cambridge MA: Harvard University Press, 2002.

Lenhoff, Howard. *Black Jews, Jews, and Other Heroes: How Grassroots Activism Led to the Rescue of the Ethiopian Jews*. Jerusalem: Gefen Publishing House, 2007.

Lerner, Michael, and Cornel West. *Jews and Blacks: A Dialogue on Race, Religion, and Culture in America*. New York: Plume, 1995.

———. *Jews and Blacks: Let the Healing Begin*. New York: Putnam's Son, 1995.

Leslau, Wolf. *Falasha Anthology: The Black Jews of Ethiopia*. New York: Schocken Books, 1969.

Lester, Julius. "The Lives People Live." In Berman, *Blacks and Jews*, 164–77.

Levine, Hillel, and Lawrence Harmon. *The Death of an American Jewish Community: A Tragedy of Good Intentions*. New York: Free Press, 1992.

Lewis, David Levering. "Parallels and Divergences: Assimilationist Strategies of Afro-Americans and Jewish Elites from 1910 to the Early 1930s." *Journal of American History* 71 (1984): 543–64.

———. "Parallels and Divergences: Assimilationist Strategies of Afro-American and Jewish Elites from 1910 to the Early 1930s." In Adams and Bracey, *Strangers and Neighbors*, 331–35.

———. "Shortcuts to the Mainstream: Afro-American and Jewish Notables in the 1920s and 1930s." In Washington, *Jews in Black Perspectives*, 90.

Lloyd, Vincent. "Introduction: Managing Race, Managing Religion." In *Race and Secularism in America*, edited by Jonathan Kahn and Vincent Lloyd, 1–19. New York: Columbia University Press, 2016.

Locke, Hubert, ed. *The Black Anti-Semitism Controversy: Protestant Views and Perspectives*. Selinsgrove PA: Susquehanna University Press, Associated University Presses, 1994.

Lubin, Alex. *Geographies of Liberation: The Making of an Afro-Arab Political Imaginary*. Chapel Hill: University of North Carolina Press, 2014.

Maffly-Kipp, Laurie. *Setting down the Sacred Past: African-American Race Histories*. Cambridge MA: Belknap Press of Harvard University Press, 2010.

Malamud, Bernard. *The Tenants*. New York: Farrar, Straus and Giroux, 1971.

Marbury, Herbert R. *Pillars of Cloud and Fire: The Politics of Exodus in African American Biblical Interpretation*. New York: New York University Press, 2015.

Martin, Tony. *The Jewish Onslaught: Despatches from the Wellesley Battlefront*. Dover MA: Majority Press, 1993.

Marx, Karl, and Friedrich Engels. *The Marx-Engels Reader*. Edited by Robert C. Tucker. New York: Norton, 1972.

McBride, James. *The Color of Water: A Black Man's Tribute to His White Mother*. New York: Riverhead Books, 2006.

McSweeney, Leah, and Jacob Siegel. "Is the Women's March Melting Down?" *Tablet Magazine*, December 10, 2018. https://www.tabletmag.com/sections/news/articles/is-the-womens-march-melting-down.

Michaeli, Ethan. "Another Exodus: The Hebrew Israelites from Chicago to Dimona." In Chireau and Deutsch, *Black Zion*, 73–87.

Miller, Perry. "Errand into the Wilderness." *The William and Mary Quarterly* 10, no. 1 (January 1953): 4–32.

Mills, Charles. "Dark Ontologies: Blacks, Jews, and White Supremacy." In *Autonomy and Community: Readings in Contemporary Kantian Social Philosophy*, edited by Jane Kneller and Sidney Axinn, 131–68. Albany: State University of New York Press, 1998.

―――. *The Racial Contract*. New York: Cornell University Press, 1997.

Moore, Deborah Dash. "Separate Paths: Blacks and Jews in the Twentieth-Century South." In Salzman and West, *Struggles in the Promised Land*, 275–93.

Moreno, Paul. "An Ambivalent Legacy: Black Americans and the Political Economy of the New Deal." *Independent Review* 6, no. 4 (2002): 513–39.

Morgan, David. "Eugenia Levy Phillips: The Civil War Experiences of a Southern Jewish Woman." In Sarna and Mendelsohn, *Jews and the Civil War*, 267–78.

Morris, Tiyi. *Womanpower Unlimited and the Black Freedom Struggle in Mississippi*. Athens: University of Georgia Press, 2015.

Movement for Black Lives (M4BL). "Cut Military Expenditures Brief." *A Vision for Black Lives: Policy Demands for Black Power, Freedom, & Justice*, August 3, 2016. https://m4bl.org/wp-content/uploads/2020/05/CutMilitaryExpenditures OnePager.pdf.

―――. "Vision for Black Lives." August 3, 2016. https://m4bl.org/policy -platforms/.

Nash Onolemhemhen, Durrenda, and Kebede Gessesse. *The Black Jews of Ethiopia: The Last Exodus*. Lanham MD: Scarecrow Press, 1998.

Nation of Islam's Historical Research Department. *The Secret Relationship between Blacks and Jews*. Vol. 1. New York: Nation of Islam, 1991.

Newton, Zachary. *Facing Black and Jew: Literature as Public Space in Twentieth-Century America*. New York: Cambridge University Press, 1999.

Ojanuga, Durrenda. "The Ethiopian Jewish Experience as Blacks in Israel." *Journal of Black Studies* 24 (1993): 147–58.

Pagano, John-Paul. "The Women's March Has a Farrakhan Problem." *The Atlantic*, March 8, 2018. https://www.theatlantic.com/politics/archive/2018/03 /womens-march/555122/.

Paley, Grace. "Zagrowsky Tells." In *The Collected Stories*, 348–64. New York: Farrar, Straus and Giroux, 1994.

Parfitt, Tudor. *Black Jews in Africa and the Americas*. Cambridge MA: Harvard University Press, 2013.

Patterson, Robert. *Exodus Politics: Civil Rights and Leadership in African American Literature and Culture*. Charlottesville: University of Virginia Press, 2013.

Perry, Huey, and Ruth White. "The Post–Civil Rights Transformation of the Relationship between Blacks and Jews in the United States." *Phylon* 47 (1960): 51–60.

Podhoretz, Norman. "My Negro Problem—and Ours." In Berman, *Blacks and Jews*, 76–96.

Pogrebin, Letty. "Ain't We Both Women? Blacks, Jews, and Gender." In *Deborah, Golda and Me: Being Female and Jewish in America*, 275–81. New York: Crown Publishers, 1991.

———. "Anti-Semitism in the Women's Movement." *Ms. Magazine*, June 1982. https://jwa.org/media/anti-semitism-in-womens-movement-by-letty-cottin-pogrebin.

———. "Blacks, Jews, and Gender: The History, Politics and Cultural Anthropology of a Women's Dialogue Group." In Salzman and West, *Struggles in the Promised Land*, 385–400.

Pritchett, Wendell. *Brownsville, Brooklyn: Blacks, Jews, and the Changing Face of the Ghetto*. Chicago: University of Chicago Press, 2002.

Prusher, Ilene. "This Is What Democracy Looks Like." *Forward*, June 2, 2020. https://forward.com/news/447876/this-is-what-democracy-looks-like/.

Raab, Earl. "American Blacks and Israel." In *Anti-Zionism and Antisemitism in the Contemporary World*, edited by Robert S. Wistrich, 155–70. London: Palgrave Macmillan, 1990.

Raboteau, Albert J. *A Fire in the Bones: Reflections on African-American Religious History*. Boston: Beacon Press, 1995.

Redkey, Edwin S. *Black Exodus: Black Nationalist and Back-to-Africa Movements, 1890–1910*. New Haven CT: Yale University Press, 1969.

Reed, Adolph, Jr. "Blacks and Jews in Democratic Coalition." In Adams and Bracey, *Strangers and Neighbors*, 729–40.

———. "What Color Is Anti-Semitism?" In Adams and Bracey, *Strangers and Neighbors*, 24–26.

Rickford, Russell. "Black Lives Matter: Toward a Modern Practice of Mass Struggle." *New Labor Forum* 25, no. 1 (January 1, 2016): 34–42.

Rinn, Miriam. "Black Jews: Changing the Face of American Jewry." *The Reporter: Women's American ORT* 45 (1995): 10–14.

Rogow, Faith. *Gone to Another Meeting: The National Council of Jewish Women, 1893–1993*. Tuscaloosa: The University of Alabama Press, 1993.

Rose, Peter. "Blacks and Jews: The Strained Alliance." *Annals of the American Academy of Political and Social Science* 454 (1981): 55–69.

———, ed. *Ghetto and Beyond: Essays on Jewish Life in America*. New York: Random House, 1969.

Rosen, Robert. "Jewish Confederates." In Sarna and Mendelsohn, *Jews and the Civil War*, 227–52.

Rosenfeld, Alvin H., and Moshe Davis. "Promised Land(s): Zion, America, and American Jewish Writers." *Jewish Social Studies*, New Series, 3, no. 3 (1997): 111–31.

Rothberg, Michael. *The Implicated Subject: Beyond Victims and Perpetrators*. Stanford CA: Stanford University Press, 2019.

Rubin, Gary. "African Americans and Israel." In Salzman and West, *Struggles in the Promised Land*, 357–70.

Ruchames, Louis. "The Abolitionists and the Jews: Some Further Thoughts." In Sarna and Mendelsohn, *Jews and the Civil War*, 145–66.

Said, Edward. "Michael Walzer's 'Exodus and Revolution': A Canaanite Reading." *Grand Street* 5, no. 2 (Winter 1986): 86–106.

Salzman, Jack. "Struggles in the Promised Land." In Salzman and West, *Struggles in the Promised Land*, 1–20.

Salzman, Jack, and Cornel West, eds. *Struggles in the Promised Land: Toward a History of Black-Jewish Relations in the United States*. New York: Oxford, 1997.

Sarna, Jonathan D., and Adam Mendelsohn, eds. *Jews and the Civil War: A Reader*. New York: New York University Press, 2010.

Schachner, Hollis, Sara Stock Mayo, and Rachel Stock Spilker. "Aleinu. It Is on Us." *Forward*, May 29, 2020. https://forward.com/scribe/447682/aleinu-it-is-on-us/.

Schoem, David, and Marshall Stevenson. "Teaching Ethnic Identity and Intergroup Relations: The Case of Black-Jewish Dialogue." In Adams and Bracey, *Strangers and Neighbors*, 823–36.

Schraub, David. "White Jews: An Intersectional Approach." *AJS Review* 43 (2019): 379–407.

Schultz, Debra L. *Going South: Jewish Women in the Civil Rights Movement*. New York: New York University Press, 2002.

Shankman, Arnold. *Ambivalent Friends: Afro-Americans View the Immigrant*. Westport CT: Greenwood Press, 1982.

Shapiro, Edward. *Crown Heights: Blacks, Jews, and the 1991 Brooklyn Riot*. Waltham MA: Brandeis University Press, 2006.

Shapiro, Emily. "Charleston Shooting: A Timeline of Events." ABC News, June 18, 2015. https://abcnews.go.com/US/charleston-shooting-happened-inside-church/story?id=31855652.

Shulman, George. *American Prophecy: Race and Redemption in American Political Culture*. Minneapolis: University of Minnesota Press, 2008.

Sicher, Efraim, ed. *Race, Color, Identity: Rethinking Discourses about "Jews" in the Twenty-First Century*. New York: Berghahn Books, 2013.

Silverman, Jason. "The Law of the Land Is the Law: Antebellum Jews, Slavery, and the Old South." In Salzman and West, *Struggles in the Promised Land*, 73–86.

Singer, Merrill. "Symbolic Identity Formation in an African-American Religious Sect." In Chireau and Deutsch, *Black Zion*, 55–72.

Sklar, Richard. "Africa and the Middle East: What Blacks and Jews Owe to Each Other." In Washington, *Jews in Black Perspectives*, 132–47.

Smith, Barbara. "Between a Rock and a Hard Place: Relationships between Black and Jewish Women." In Adams and Bracey, *Strangers and Neighbors*, 765–80.

———. "A Rock and a Hard Place: Relationships between Black and Jewish Women." *Women's Studies Quarterly* 11, no. 3 (1983): 7–9.

Smith, Rogers. "Religious Rhetoric and the Ethics of Public Discourse: The Case of George W. Bush." *Political Theory* 36 (2008): 272–300.

Sobel, B. Z., and May Sobel. "Negroes and Jews: American Minority Groups in Conflict." In Rose, *Ghetto and Beyond*, 384–408.

Sokolow, Jayme. "Revolution and Reform: The Antebellum Jewish Abolitionists." In Sarna and Mendelsohn, *Jews and the Civil War*, 125–44.

St. Clair Drake, John Gibbs. "African Diaspora and Jewish Diaspora: Convergence and Divergence." In Washington, *Jews in Black Perspectives*, 19–41.

Stewart, Maria W. *Maria W. Stewart: America's First Black Woman Political Writer: Essays and Speeches.* Edited by Marilyn Richardson. Bloomington: Indiana University Press, 1987.

Student Nonviolent Coordinating Committee (SNCC). "Third World Round-up: The Palestine Problem: Test Your Knowledge." *SNCC Newsletter* 1, no. 2 (July–August 1967): 5–6.

Sundquist, Eric J. *Strangers in the Land: Blacks, Jews, Post-Holocaust America.* Cambridge MA: Belknap Press, 2005.

Terry, Janice. "The Carter Administration and the Palestinians." *Arab Studies Quarterly* 12 (1990): 153–65.

Tighe, Elizabeth, Raquel Magidin de Kramer, Daniel Parmer, Daniel Nussbaum, Daniel Kallista, Xajavion Seabrum, and Leonard Saxe. "American Jewish Population Project: Summary and Highlights 2019." Waltham MA: Brandeis University Steinhardt Social Research Institute, 2019. https://ajpp.brandeis.edu/documents/2019/JewishPopulationDataBrief2019.pdf.

Tobin, Diana, Gary Tobin, and Scott Rubin. *In Every Tongue: The Racial and Ethnic Diversity of the Jewish People.* San Francisco: Institute for Jewish and Community Research, 2005.

Tobin, Jonathan. "The Anti-Israel Left and the Dems." *Commentary*, August 9, 2016. https://www.commentarymagazine.com/jonathan-tobin/the-anti-israel-left-and-the-dems/.

Trotter, Joe, Jr. "African Americans, Jews, and the City: Perspectives from the Industrial Era." In Franklin et al., *African Americans and Jews*, 193–207.

Vorspan, Albert. "Blacks and Jews." In Hentoff, *Black Anti-Semitism*, 191–228.

Walker, Alice. *Meridian*. Orlando: Harvest, 1976.

Walker, Rebecca. *Black, White, and Jewish: Autobiography of a Shifting Self*. New York: Riverhead, 2001.

Walters, Ronald. "The Young Resignation: What Does It Mean?" *New Directions* 7, no. 1 (1979): 7–14.

Walzer, Michael. *Exodus and Revolution*. New York: Basic Books, 1985.

Walzer, Michael, and Edward W. Said. "An Exchange: 'Exodus and Revolution.'" *Grand Street* 5, no. 4 (1986): 246–59.

Washington, Booker T. *The Future of the American Negro*. Boston: Small, Maynard, 1900. http://library.um.edu.mo/ebooks/b17839063.pdf.

Washington, Joseph R., Jr., ed. *Jews in Black Perspectives: A Dialogue*. Cranbury NJ: Associated University Presses, 1984.

Webb, Clive. *Fight against Fear: Southern Jews and Black Civil Rights*. Athens: University of Georgia Press, 2001.

Weisbord, Robert, and Richard Kazarian Jr. *Israel in the Black American Perspective*. Westport CT: Greenwood Press, 1985.

Weisbord, Robert, and Arthur Stein. *Bittersweet Encounter: The Afro-American and the American Jew*. Westport CT: Negro Universities Press, 1970.

Weiss, Nancy. "Long-Distance Runners of the Civil Rights Movement: The Contribution of Jews to the NAACP and the National Urban League in the Early Twentieth Century." In Salzman and West, *Struggles in the Promised Land*, 123–52.

West, Cornel. "On Black-Jewish Relations." In Berman, *Blacks and Jews*, 144–53.

Wexler, Ellen. "American Jewish Groups Respond to the Movement for Black Lives' Platform." *Moment Magazine*, August 9, 2016. https://momentmag.com/black-lives-matters-stance-on-israel/.

Wilkerson, Isabel. *The Warmth of Other Suns: The Epic Story of America's Great Migration*. New York: Random House, 2010.

Williams, Delores. *Sisters in the Wilderness: The Challenge of Womanist God-talk*. Maryknoll NY: Orbis Books, 1993.

Williams, Patricia. "On Imagining Foes, Imagining Friendship." In Salzman and West, *Struggles in the Promised Land*, 371–83.

Willis, Ellen. "The Myth of the Powerful Jew." In Berman, *Blacks and Jews*, 183–203.

Wimbush, Vincent. "Reading Texts through Worlds, Worlds through Texts." *Semeia* 61 (1993).

Winter, Tom, Dennis Romero, and Saphora Smith, "How a Deadly Shooting Unfolded at Tree of Life Synagogue in Pittsburgh." NBC News, October 28, 2018. https://www.nbcnews.com/news/us-news/tree-life-synagogue-deadly-shooting-n925291.

Wolfson, Bernard. "African American Jews: Dispelling Myths, Bridging the Divide." In Chireau and Deutsch, *Black Zion*, 33–54.

Wright, Richard. *Uncle Tom's Children*. New York: HarperPerennial, 2004.

INDEX

ABOUT THE AUTHORS

Jacques Berlinerblau is a professor of Jewish civilization in the Walsh School of Foreign Service at Georgetown University. He is the author of ten books, including *How to Be Secular: A Call to Arms for Religious Freedom* (Houghton Mifflin Harcourt, 2012), *The Secular Bible: Why Nonbelievers Must Take Religion Seriously* (Cambridge University Press, 2005), and *Heresy in the University: The Black Athena Controversy and the Responsibilities of American Intellectuals* (Rutgers University Press, 1999). He has appeared as a commentator on culture, religion, and politics for outlets such as the *Washington Post, Chronicle of Higher Education, The Forward, Salon*, NPR, CNN, and PBS, among others. His next book is *The Philip Roth We Don't Know: Sex, Race, Autobiography* (University of Virginia Press, 2021).

Terrence L. Johnson is an associate professor of religion and politics in the Department of Government, an affiliate faculty member of the Department of African American Studies, and a senior faculty fellow at the Berkley Center for Religion, Peace, and World Affairs at Georgetown University. He is the author of *We Testify with Our Lives: How Religion Transformed Radical Thought from Black Power to Black Lives Matter* (Columbia University Press, 2021) and *Tragic Soul-Life: W. E. B. Du Bois and the Moral Crisis Facing American Democracy* (Oxford University Press, 2012). He is also coeditor of the Religious Cultures of African and African Diaspora People book series at Duke University Press.

A graduate of Morehouse College, Johnson received his master of divinity from Harvard Divinity School and doctorate in religious studies from Brown University.